Crime, Clemency & Consequence in Britain 1821–39

Crime, Clemency & Consequence in Britain 1821–39

A Slice of Criminal Life

Alison Eatwell

PEN & SWORD
HISTORY

First published in Great Britain in 2017 by
Pen & Sword History
an imprint of
Pen & Sword Books Ltd
47 Church Street
Barnsley
South Yorkshire
S70 2AS

ISBN 978 1 47383 031 8

A CIP catalogue record for this book is
available from the British Library.

Printed and bound in England
by CPI Group (UK) Ltd, Croydon CR0 4YY

Pen & Sword Books Ltd incorporates the Imprints of Pen & Sword Books
Archaeology, Atlas, Aviation, Battleground, Discovery, Family History, History,
Maritime, Military, Naval, Politics, Railways, Select, Transport, True Crime,
Fiction, Frontline Books, Leo Cooper, Praetorian Press, Seaforth Publishing,
Wharncliffe and White Owl.

For a complete list of Pen & Sword titles please contact
PEN & SWORD BOOKS LIMITED
47 Church Street, Barnsley, South Yorkshire, S70 2AS, England
E-mail: enquiries@pen-and-sword.co.uk
Website: www.pen-and-sword.co.uk

Contents

Acknowledgements

With thanks to the staff and volunteer editors and cataloguers working on the 'HO17 Criminal Petitions for Mercy Project' at the National Archives, Kew, in particular Briony Paxman, Colin Williams, Celia Cartwright, Brenda Mortimer, Barry Purdon and Anne Wheeldon. Thanks also to Roy Metcalfe and Mac Mowat.

Old Bailey Online - The Proceedings of the Old Bailey, 1674–1913, has been used for background reading and as research for specific Old Bailey cases. Where appropriate, case reference numbers are included in the End Notes.

Textual Conventions

Throughout the text the following conventions have been applied:

I have used the term 'Home Secretary' in place of 'Principal Secretary for the Home Department' to ensure standardisation amongst the petitions. 'Home Office' is used throughout in the place of 'Home Department' for the same reason.

Where variations in the spelling of names have been found, the different versions have been noted, but thereafter a single spelling has been used, except if the name appears within a quotation.

Unless it is clear where a case is located, or if otherwise stated within the petitions and documents sent, I have added the current city to situate an address where only street names have been given by letter-writers eg. London.

Spelling and grammar, within quotes, is that used by the sender. However, some quotations may have been modernised to make the sense accessible while retaining their original meaning.

Introduction

Historians have often used Court and Home Office records to reconstruct the key events in a prisoner's life, but these documents rarely reveal the level of incidental detail or personal circumstance which allows us to view the prisoner as an individual reacting in a dynamic world. However, The National Archives in Kew, Surrey, holds thousands of petitions from the earlier decades of the nineteenth century. These petitions, from prisoners, their families, employers, supporters or even prosecutors, were written after the prisoner had been sentenced, in the hope of gaining a commutation of their punishment.

Held in series HO17 and HO18 the petitions are a unique and exciting source of rare glimpses in to everyday routines, working conditions, illnesses, relationships, foreigners in Britain, Britons transported overseas, and life in a locality. They are sometimes accompanied by witness statements and other supporting documentation. By using these primary sources, this book hopes to bring to life some of the individuals caught in the justice system and show how they responded to the position in which they found themselves, providing a flavour of criminal activity at the time.

The individual cases in this book are taken from HO17 (and associated documentation), and this series contains around twenty thousand petitions in total. Whilst the petitions here do not claim to be statistically representative of the series – and indeed it is not certain how many petitions received by the Home Office were later misfiled or otherwise not included – they begin to illustrate the breadth of issues and differing criminal activity in the 1820s and 1830s, the wide range of people involved and the legal procedures at the time. They are all unified by one thing at least; they are written by people who were strongly motivated, and often desperate, to take the time and bear the cost to appeal for a reduction in their own or their loved-one's sentence. Although some prisoners claim to be innocent, all here had been found guilty and sentenced as such. These are cases in which people had much to lose and much to gain.

This book also allows us to consider how much, or how little, has changed in the types of crime committed, the circumstances and those committing them. It also demonstrates how human emotions remain constant across the centuries and shows that many of the background social and political situations have resonance today.

At the heart of the book, in all senses, are the letters and paperwork which show private feelings and personal details. Read as individual cases, each subject is fascinating; viewed together, the collection reveals a unique and often unexpected insight in to life in 1820s and 1830s Britain.

Chapter 1

Situating the Petitions:
A Brief Overview of the 1820s and 1830s

According to the 1821 census, England and Wales had a population of 12,000,236, Scotland 2,091,521 and Ireland 6,801,827. By the 1841 census, the figures had risen to 15,914,148 for England and Wales, 2,620,184 in Scotland and 8,196,598 in Ireland. Much of that population had been lured away from agriculture and in to the growing cities as people looked for work. In 1841, less than two thirds of London's residents had been born in the capital, many drawn from other parts of Europe as well England, Scotland, Wales and Ireland.

After a period of economic decline, due to demands on its finances by the Napoleonic Wars, the country experienced an economic boom in the early years of the 1820s. However, sudden recession was to follow in the middle of that decade and, with the British economy largely dependent on cotton, recession would occur again in the 1830s, though the expansion of the railways would then bring increasing stability. The Bank of England was not the only source of bank notes; many independent country banks issued their own, as did banks in Scotland and Ireland. But many smaller banks were unable to withstand the challenging conditions and in the years following the financial crisis in 1825 and 1826, the Bank of England began to open branches outside the capital in a move to help stabilise the currency.

In art, the first half of the nineteenth century saw a return to themes of personal experience and emotional response, especially where nature was concerned. In 1821, John Constable painted *The Hay Wain* and the following year, George IV commissioned J.M.W. Turner to paint a large picture of *The Battle of Trafalgar* which he delivered in 1824. It was presented to the Naval Gallery in Greenwich Hospital in 1829.

In the theatre, Drury Lane, Covent Garden and the patent theatres monopolised the English classics until the Theatre Regulation Act of 1843 allowed other theatres to present plays. In these other theatres, domestic melodrama found popularity, often based on real events and recent crimes. In November 1823, The Surrey theatre in London staged the Thurtell-Weare murder case under the title *The Gamblers*, using the murderer's furniture on stage. The run was halted by order of the Court of Kings Bench, which considered the piece drew too heavily on actual events, but it was re-staged early the following year.[1] The petition of **Joseph Hunt**, convicted of aiding and abetting John Thurtell in murdering William Weare, is within the HO17 series. Many self-penned versions of *Maria Marten or the Murder in the Red Barn* were played nationwide, as soon as the crime became public knowledge in 1827. In 1829, *Black-Ey'd Susan* by Douglas Jerrold, 'the father of nautical melodrama',[2] had its first production at The Surrey.

Child stars, playing adult roles, were hugely popular throughout these decades. Clara Fisher was perhaps one of the best known, playing Shylock and Richard III before changing to female roles as she grew older. She emigrated to America and established an enduring career, unlike some of her child contemporaries.

The written word saw the first publication of *Confessions of an Opium Eater* by Thomas de Quincey, in the *London Magazine* in 1821. Fifteen years later, the serial publication began of Dickens' *The Pickwick Papers* with *Oliver Twist* to follow in 1837 and *Nicholas Nickleby* the year after.

John Keats died in 1821 (at the age of 25), and Percy Bysshe Shelley and George Gordon, Lord Byron, died in 1822 and 1824 respectively. Alfred, Lord Tennyson published a volume of poetry which included *The Lady of Shalott* in 1833.

In 1822, the Academy of Music was established, receiving its Royal Charter in 1830.

George IV had come to the throne in 1820 and would be succeeded by William IV in 1830, followed by Victoria in 1837. Ten different Principal Secretaries to the Home Department, now commonly called 'Home Secretary', served in this period and these would be the men to whom petitions for mercy were sent. Robert Peel, later Sir Robert Peel, served twice. See Appendix 1.

In 1829, the Metropolitan Police Act lead to the establishment of a 3,000-man centralised force, to police the metropolitan area, excluding the City of London. This force reported to the Home Secretary and focused on crime prevention. Its numbers were increased to 4,300 men in the second Metropolitan Police Act ten years later, and its area of power extended to fifteen miles from Charing Cross. A separate detective force was later created to work alongside the officers on the streets.

In 1832, the first Reform Act or Great Reform Act introduced long awaited changes to the electoral system in England and Wales. It increased the electorate to around 650,000, almost doubling the number of men able to vote. But whilst it began to address the un-representative and unbalanced elections which preceded it, women and the large majority of working men still had no vote. Still without a secret ballot, voters were open to enticement and intimidation.

The 1820s saw the beginning of the centralisation, standardisation and bureaucratisation of English criminal law, with parochial powers being removed. This process continued in the 1830s as the 'Bloody Code' was over-hauled. The number of crimes which carried the death penalty was gradually reduced, a process started by Sir Samuel Romilly and Robert Peel. With the Judgement of Death Act in 1823, the mandatory death penalty became discretionary for all crimes other than murder or treason. Although death sentences were necessarily entered on court records, judges were able to reduce sentencing at trial, although some prisoners found guilty would enjoy no reduction in order to deter other would-be offenders. However, judges at the Old Bailey did not have this discretion; instead the decisions were taken by the King in Council where serious cases were discussed. Under the Murder Act of 1752, execution had to take place two days after sentencing, or three if sentencing was on a Friday. In 1834, this would increase to ensure a minimum of two Sundays elapsed. There was little time to raise a petition, but if the prisoner could show there was false evidence against them or new information found, they might hope for respite for a week.

The two types of offences, misdemeanours and felonies, were dealt with in different courts. Misdemeanours were tried in Petty Sessions, and sometimes, though not often, at Courts of Quarter Sessions. Felonies were tried at Courts of Quarter Sessions and Courts of Assize, most felonies being capital and thus carrying the death penalty. The Old Bailey was the Assize Court for London and until 1834 had jurisdiction over crimes committed in the City of London (but no part of London south of the Thames) and Middlesex. In 1834, it became the Central Criminal Court and its jurisdiction changed; for the next 130 years it would cover London, Middlesex, parts of Essex, Kent and Surrey, and those offences previously tried at Admiralty Sessions. English law was administered in Wales and the Court of Great Sessions in Wales heard felonies and serious misdemeanours, except those committed in Monmouthshire and heard on the Oxford Assize circuit, until it was abolished in 1830. Each of the Assizes had two sittings in spring and summer; the Old Bailey had eight sessions per year. Different judges attended different circuits and thus gained knowledge of the area. A chairman and magistrates also sat on the bench.

Although Scotland had a different justice system, influenced by Roman law, a small number of Scottish petitions are included in HO17 series as well as English and Welsh cases, with occasional ones from the Isle of Man and the Channel islands. The Scottish court system differed, for instance, in having Sheriff's Courts, Circuit Courts and High Courts, and its criminals could be tried for offences that did not exist in England and Wales, including 'theft (habit and repute)' and 'stouthrief'.[3] Other differences included married female criminals being referred to by their maiden names, fifteen people on a jury at the start of a trial, and the alternative verdict of 'not proven'.

The Process of Mercy and Petitions

The early 1820s penal system in Britain was regarded as the most severe in Europe and by 1822 over 200 crimes were punishable by death. However, this number had grown in the absence of any centralised strategy regarding the development of offences and only a minority of these capital offences were ever prosecuted. The process was also mitigated by the use of discretion.

Although the law would be rationalised over the next twenty years and those elements which have since been called the 'Bloody Code' would be repealed, the Court of Criminal Appeal would not be constituted until the next century. The Court of Appeal of England and Wales was created in 1875 following the Judicature Commission recommending reforms to the justice system. The Court of Criminal Appeal was established in 1907 and heard appeals on both the verdict and the sentence of criminal cases.

With no statutory right of appeal against either verdict or sentence and with sentences including Death and the more prevalent Transportation, the prisoner had much to lose. Mercy was a continuation of the legal process but was not something to which the prisoner had the right. Mercy could take the form of either a reduction in sentence or the granting of a pardon, pardons forming a part of the rationalisation of the law regarding capital convictions. Petitions against criminal convictions could not ask for 'justice' but they could appeal for mercy.

In law, all indictments were considered an offence against the Crown and only the Crown could grant mercy. Since the establishment of the Home Office in 1782, the royal prerogative was exercised through the Home Secretary and by the early nineteenth century a large part of the Home Office's work was dealing with such petitions. With the same monarch as England and Wales, although with a different Court system, Scottish petitions had to be sent to the Home Secretary, as did those from the Isle of Man and Courts Martial. At this time, all correspondence was reviewed by the Home Secretary himself, with the help and expertise of his staff and the clerks who summarised the contents of the case on the outside of the paperwork. To help the Home Secretary make his decision, a comment from the relevant local gaoler was added by the clerks, which at times differed from the character painted by the petitioner.

Petitions for mercy on behalf of a prisoner could be sent by supporters, or the prisoner themselves, at any point after sentencing. Requests were not restricted by severity of sentence nor number of times the sentence had been mitigated, and there was no limit to the number of requests a petitioner could make, except perhaps the cost involved to those sending them. In 1834, **Mary Byrne**, 'upward of 50 years' old was tried at Lancaster Quarter Sessions for Receiving Stolen Goods. Found guilty she was sentenced to two years imprisonment with hard labour. On three occasions Mary Byrne's husband Patrick petitioned to have his wife released and her daughter Mary Nowland petitioned thirteen times. All were without success.

A petition could be sent from a single person or from scores of friends and neighbours, and could take the form of a single page or several pages of detailed information with reasons for mitigation. To enhance their chances of success, petitioners often sought the support of, or requested the forwarding of the petition via, the most respectable person they could access. For most this would be a clergyman or local MP who might not know the prisoner but might vouch for the respectability of some of the signatories to the petition. This route was not only used in an effort to make the prisoner appear respectable, but was pragmatic; the answer filtered back through the person who presented the petition to the Home Office and the request might receive a reply quicker than might otherwise be the case. **Thomas Allen** (or **Allan**) was able to go a step further when he was found guilty of embezzlement at Essex Winter Assizes and sentenced to fourteen years transportation in 1832. Allen, a 42-year-old farming bailiff, had worked for Lady Laura Tollemache and appealed to her in two letters sent from Springfield Gaol, Chelmsford, Essex, stating how being in her service 'made me look up to you for your Humanity'. Her family connections ensured Allen's letters were passed via Lord Dysart to the brother of the Home Secretary and considered with a petition sent by fifty-nine local people. Allen was then ordered to the General Penitentiary, Millbank in London, the Home Office annotation adding 'if he behaves well, his Term of 14 years will be reduced'.

Reasons offered as grounds for clemency were many and varied. It was often claimed that the prisoner was innocent or unaware they were committing a crime. Frequently it was stated this was the prisoner's first offence before which they had an excellent character. Although this was sometimes true, other prisoners relied on inefficient checking systems to hide their previous bad practices; names were often changed or variously spelt and written descriptions of physical image were of limited value. One's 'character' was hugely important at a time when many people dealt in trade; one's word, honour and reputation needed protection when word-of-mouth recommendations were vital to earning a living. To this end, many prisoners were convicted under an alias which would also deflect shame from them or their family. As the population grew in the metropolis and cities such as Birmingham and Manchester, the anonymity the large crowds afforded was a two-edged sword. It might be easier for a criminal to commit a crime but his or her worth might be less than that within a smaller community where they played a vital role providing goods or services and the community were more willing to deal with the offender by means other than prosecution.

Ill-health, mental instability or old age would make a prisoner undesirable or expensive to any receiver overseas and such claims were used in petitions in the hope of avoiding transportation. Whilst youth might be a more attractive trait to those with one eye on building a new colony or needing workers for the naval docks in Bermuda, it was also used by the petitioner as a reason why the prisoner was involved in a crime, drawn in through naivety or being duped by bad company.

The age of the prisoner often differs between petitions and other records. Exact age was an uncertain fact for many, not just for the criminal classes. Prior to 1837, incomplete parish registers were the only indicator and baptism, one measure, could take place at any time. Civil registration of births, marriages and deaths was introduced in England and Wales on 1 July 1837 and almost 20 years later in Scotland. Irish non-Catholic marriages were registered from 1845 and all births marriages and deaths from 1864. Suspicion of the new system led to many failing to register. In an effort to gain more sympathy in petitions, ages were almost certainly reduced for girls and youths; for those older, ages were over-estimated to suggest increasing infirmity and dwindling use overseas. It was common practice at this time to describe age differently. Those who nowadays would be considered to be 18 for example, would be considered as being in their nineteenth year and thus '19'.

A very real consideration for many was the reliance of the prisoner's family upon their wages, without which dependents would be left destitute and claims of this are frequent. Many petitions stated an offer of employment had been secured should the prisoner be released, which not only would mean the offender would be a useful member of society again, but the family would not have to be supported by parish relief.

Events surrounding or during the trial were often cited as grounds for clemency, including unreliable witnesses. Attorneys were accused of being negligent and prosecutors of being criminals themselves, as with the case of **John Horrocks**, who was convicted of stealing from the person at Lancaster Quarter Sessions in 1833 and received a sentence of fourteen years transportation. Amongst the papers sent to the Home Office were depositions attesting to the bad character of the prosecutor, Peter Whittle, who was in gaol for theft by that time. Often trials were brought forward, making it difficult or expensive for character witnesses to attend, even if the prisoner had an opportunity to tell their supporters the trial was to take place at all. In such cases, supporting character references were sent to the Home Office along with the prisoner's petition.

Occasionally petitions are more ambitious in their reasons for clemency. One instance of very speculative petitioning was that sent supporting the cases of **Alexander Lowry**, **John Lowry**, **Joseph Kayle**, **Jane Kayle**, **William Colquhoun**, **Thomas Caine**, **John Cammell**, and **John Clague**, in October 1827. Details of the court and trial dates are not given. The Home Office Clerk describes their crime only as 'various misdemeanours' and the sentence as 'various terms of imprisonment', but the prisoners were in the gaol at Castle Rushen on the Isle of Man. The reason for clemency was to mark the King's acquisition of manorial rights over the island from the Duke of Athol. Unsurprisingly the petition is marked 'refused'.

Some petitions ask the reader to stretch their belief. **William Wakefield** was tried for aiding and abetting his brother, Edward, in abducting the fifteen-year-old heiress and daughter of the High Sheriff, Ellen Turner. She had been tricked, the prosecution said, into an elopement at Gretna Green. Wakefield was convicted at Lancaster Lent Assizes in 1827 and faced three years imprisonment. He petitioned, in December 1828, with supporting signatures from eighteen people, giving amongst his reasons for clemency that he was unaware he was involved in an elopement to Gretna Green. Although Wakefield was sitting in the dickey seat of a carriage with his brother and Miss Turner, he claimed he did not know that she was being deceived by his brother, Edward. Despite his petition being forwarded in a supporting letter from Lord Stanley, William Wakefield's petition's is annotated as follows:

'Pray look at the printed trial – I believe that the statement of the prisoner to be inconsistent in many respects with the evidence on which he was convicted.'

Petitions were not always in support of the prisoner. Some petitioners urged the Home Secretary to stand firm; they wished an example to be made to the community as a deterrent, or wanted to rid their area of those they considered to be bad influences or troublesome characters, as did seven magistrates in Wiltshire. Well-known poacher **Isaac Hatherell** had 'corrupted the youth of the town of Chippenham' and when he was convicted of offences against the game laws at the Wiltshire Lent Assizes, 1834, the magistrates tried to ensure he served the seven year transportation sentence he received.

John McKennil (or **McKinnell**), an assistant overseer, was tried in Halifax Magistrates Court, December 1833 and imprisoned until he paid a £50 fine imposed for failing to deliver up a parish account book. Claiming he'd handed the book over some months earlier, McKennil and his supporters petitioned the Home Secretary for his release, but the vicar and parish officers of Liversedge, West Riding of Yorkshire, were adamant he should produce the book before being let off the fine. They wrote to the Home Secretary to say so.

23-year-old **Richard Edwards** was transported for life after being tried at Cardigan Lent Assizes, 1834, and found guilty of cutting and maiming an excise officer. Edwards and his many supporters petitioned the Home Office seeking a pardon based on his good conduct and recommendations. However, the prosecutor, William Jenkins, feared reprisals and petitioned the Home Office against allowing the prisoner to return to this country.

Prisoners often petitioned to be sent to the General Penitentiary at Millbank, in preference to the notorious hulk prison ships. Not only would the prisoner learn a skill there, for example, tailoring, but their chances of staying in England increased, regardless of their original sentence. Over time, custom and practice would mean a prisoner could expect to be imprisoned in the Penitentiary a maximum of five years, despite the nature or length of their original sentence. Opportunities to demonstrate reform seemed greater at Millbank, but it is possible the prisoners selected to go there were those considered to be more capable of reform in the first place.

If a pardon was thought appropriate by the Home Office, it would be deemed to be 'prepared' for the monarch to rubber stamp, the ability to grant a pardon laying exclusively with the Crown. However, unless there was new evidence most petitions were not granted, the case marked 'Nil' and the sentence unchanged.

Chapter 2

Bigamy

Prior to the 1857 Matrimonial Causes Act, the complexity and considerable expense involved in obtaining a divorce put it out of the reach of most ordinary people; the private Act of Parliament needed was not a viable consideration. Those wishing to end a difficult marriage often reached an agreement between themselves, usually financially based. In some instances, wives were exchanged, whilst in rare cases, for an unlucky spouse, the marriage ended in the murder of one partner.

Unreliable communication links and lengthy absences by those engaged in some services, trades and professions, could make it difficult to ascertain if a spouse was alive. This was also a convenient fact of life if a change of partner was desired. It was not uncommon, then, for a person to have two living spouses and when relatives prosecuted for bigamy, it was usually in cases where money was at stake.

Petitions received by the Home Office, from those convicted of bigamy, often cite bad behaviour by a spouse, bad advice from a third party, or ignorance of any legal wrongdoing amongst their reasons for clemency.

In 1829, **Arthur Malcolm** wrote that whilst he was on army service, his first wife, Jean Smith, had lived with another man. Not only did she have children by this second man, who was now deceased, but also by a third. Malcolm claimed he believed her behaviour released him from the vows he had taken and this belief had been confirmed by a church minister who unfortunately had since died. Despite the fact Malcolm had already served half of his twelve month imprisonment, he received no reduction in the sentence passed on him at Aberdeen Circuit Court in September 1828.

John Penson considered that he had made a formal arrangement with his first wife Ann, in their mutual, written agreement to end their marriage. This, he believed, left him free to marry Eliza Brown in September 1832, having married Ann nee Wootton less than five years earlier. However, after marrying his first wife, Penson had spent time in Quebec and when he returned the couple decided they should end their marriage. Petitioning from Maidstone Gaol in May 1833, Penson stated he and his wife had become reconciled and would go to one of the new settlements if he were freed from the one year sentence imposed on him at Kent Winter Assizes, December 1832. His petition was unsuccessful.

For some convicted of bigamy, the claim that their first spouse had a bad character was supported by external evidence. **William Craig**, a travelling merchant, was convicted at the Perth Circuit Court, in April 1837. Almost four years before his trial he had married Mary Gray, but his first wife, Margaret McCallum, was still living. During his imprisonment in Montrose Gaol in Angus, Craig sent two petitions hoping for a mitigation of his seven month sentence. He stated that McCallum was a criminal who had received a sentence of transportation. Indeed, Tasmanian Archives show 'Margaret McCallum or Craig' was transported for seven years, guilty of theft, and arrived in Van Diemen's Land in January 1838 on the *Atwick* transport ship. This conviction at Perth Court in April 1837 was not her first and she had a record of bad conduct and violent behaviour. Born in Edinburgh, her age on arrival in Van Diemen's Land is stated as 28 and she died in January 1845.

William Craig gave additional reasons to support his plea for mercy: he was ignorant of the legal consequences of marrying Mary Gray; had a young family dependent upon him; and had served more than half of his sentence. However, Craig was unsuccessful, receiving 'Nil' reduction in his sentence from the Home Secretary.

Although bad behaviour by the prisoner's spouse was a reason cited for clemency, the previous behaviour of the petitioner themselves would have doubtless influenced the Home Secretary's decision. **John Machenery**, alias **John Lillis**, claimed he had discovered his first wife, Ann Evans, was 'an abandoned woman' before he married his second, Mary Draper. Although other grounds for clemency were also proffered, the Home Secretary saw no reason to reduce the seven year transportation sentence Machenery had received at the Old Bailey in 1832. The gaoler's report, noted on the prisoner's Home Office case, would not have aided his cause – 'here before'. Tasmanian Archives show John Lillis, also known as **John McHenry**, (or John **McHenrey** or **John Mackenery**) had been previously guilty of theft. He was transported on the *Jupiter* to Van Diemen's Land, arriving in May 1833. Born in Ireland, (or possibly Liverpool), the 27 year old, was employed as a labourer on arrival, appearing as Number 1559 on the Appropriation List.

As with John Machenery, the past actions of **William Pass** could not have been ignored when his petition for mercy was considered. Pass, a 20-year-old carter from Burslem, Staffordshire, was tried for bigamy before

Baron Vaughan at Staffordshire Lent Assizes, March 1828. He pleaded guilty and was sentenced to seven years transportation.

A petition was sent to the Home Secretary, on the prisoner's behalf, from nineteen inhabitants of the village of Burslem, including the Minister and Churchwardens. J.B. Marsden, the local curate, was the first signatory. Although the petition is undated, Pass is described as being on board a transport ship at Woolwich and the petitioners detail their understanding of the circumstances in which, unwittingly, Pass came to commit the offence. Pass married his first wife, Ann, when he was only 17 years old and during the latter part of the time the couple lived together, she was frequently found in the company of other men. This caused the couple to quarrel and when Ann made a false accusation against her husband, Pass was brought before Walter Weston Coyney, Justice of the Peace for Staffordshire. Coyney advised Pass to separate from his wife 'on account of her misconduct' and this Pass believed made his separation legal. The petitioners added that Ann Pass had since been discovered to be a prostitute and that Pass's parents are honest, hardworking people.

The petition from Burslem was unsuccessful; the Home Office annotation is 'to be sent abroad'. The gaoler's report states, 'Bad character, before convicted of felony. Connected with the Pottery Gang.' According to the Tasmanian Archives, William Pass was transported to Van Diemen's Land on the *Georgiana*, arriving there on April 1829.

In other examples of gaolers' reports, noted on petitions, the Pottery Gang is shown to be a gang of thieves. **John Eardley** was connected to the gang as were the Heath cousins, Lewis and Samuel. At the same Assize sitting in which Pass was convicted, 17-year-old Eardley was found guilty of stealing from a dwelling house and **Lewis Heath**, aged 17, and **Samuel Heath**, aged 18, were found guilty of highway robbery.

The bigamy case involving **Henry Napier Disney** was not only the subject of many newspapers reports but resulted in one of very few female divorces granted in the first half of the nineteenth century. Dublin-born Disney's real name was **Arthur Battersby**, but he had more recently used the name of a living, fellow Dubliner. He had been brought to face trial at the Central Criminal Court, Old Bailey, January Sessions, 1838, having married his second wife, Sarah Ann Stovin, in August of the previous year. His first wife, Ann Muckleston, was still alive; their wedding had taken place in June 1826 according to communications between the Prosecution Attorney and the Home Office, a fact that had also been established during his trial.[1] According to *The Annual Register of World Events: a Review of the Year*,[2] the defence attorney, Charles Phillips, managed to convince the court that the onus was upon the prosecution to prove the prisoner knew his first wife was alive at the time he married the second:

> 'The only evidence to prove this was given by Abraham Newland … who admitted that he had endeavoured to extort money from the prisoner for withholding his evidence.'

Despite the Common Sergeant consulting with the other judges and agreeing with Charles Phillips, the jury found the prisoner guilty. He was sentenced to seven years transportation.

Battersby, thirty at the time, was brought in to custody on 9 January 1838. The Newgate Register of Prisoners lists him as 6ft 2in tall, his occupation as labourer and notes the loss of his right arm which, he explained in his petition, was the result of battle. He was sent to the *York* hulk ship at Gosport on 12 February 1838.

The Home Office received petitions both for and against mitigation of his sentence. J.W. Dawson, Attorney for the Prosecution wrote on 8 February, pre-empting any petition from Battersby:

> 'I am in possession of facts which will prove the Prisoner to be utterly unworthy of the royal mercy, two respectable families being plunged in to irreparable distress by the unhappy marriages of the Prisoner's victims.'

However, Colonel MacDougall of the Senior United Service Club, wrote in support of Battersby on 15 March, prompted to do so because of Battersby's previous good conduct and the source of the prosecution. MacDougall states that he has seen Sarah Ann Stovin and the prosecution 'was in no manner countenanced by her, and that all proceedings were carried on by her brother in direct opposition to her wishes.'

Sarah petitioned Lord John Russell, the Home Secretary several times. On 22 May she wrote from 32, Henrietta Street, Covent Garden, requesting that he show her petition to Queen Victoria. Stovin writes that her health is failing and:

> '… it is impossible for me to bear up much longer if I am to be deprived of him whom I still and shall ever call my husband and in whose heart I can only confide all my prospects and happiness in this world, worn down with anxiety cruelly persecuted by an

unfeeling brother and his cruel associates, deprived of him who was
my only succour and protection…'

In another petition she explains she had only experienced the tenderest care
and affection from 'the best of husbands'. She signed herself S.A. Disney.

Amongst those supporting Battersby's case was John Kinlock, late
Brigadier General. He wrote on two occasions, the first sending a character reference and service record. He stresses Battersby married Sarah Ann
Stovin twelve years after he had seen or heard news of Ann Muckleston,
from whom Battersby believed he had a divorce *a mensa et thoro* and consid-
ers that might have stood 'but for a <u>recent</u> act of parliament'.

On 12 June 1838, the prosecution's attorney, J.W. Dawson, wrote again to
the Home Office in reply to a previous enquiry. Not only did Dawson state
that Battersby married Ann Muckleston in 1826, having made a deed of
settlement upon her when he had no property himself, but that:

'… he had the bad disorder which he gave to his wife, and treated
her with great cruelty which appears by the evidence produced of
her, and now filed in Doctors' Commons.'

Doctors' Commons practised civil law. Dawson continues:

'When the sentence of Divorce for Adultery and cruelty was pronounced against him, Mr Buckton of Doctors' Commons… and
Mr Shearman of Gray's Inn Square were the Proctor and Solicitor
employed on behalf of Mrs Battersby, and those gentlemen state,
that a case of greater baseness and cruelty never came before the
Court…'

He cites the expense to Mrs Battersby's father to be '£500 and upwards',
and Mr Shearman telling Mr Dawson the family did not want any mitigation of Battersby's sentence:

'– in fact if he [had] been transported for life it will have been a
good thing for the Country.'

Dawson gives further information on Battersby's actions, stating that once
Ann Muckleston and Battersby were married, he took her to Fenton's Hotel,
St James Street and incurred a Bill of £150 which he notes had still not

been paid. Battersby absconded and joined the 1st Life Guards 'as soon as it was discovered that he had diseased' Ann, and her father was intending to prosecute for divorce. However, Battersby deserted from the Regiment and later married Sarah Ann Stovin because, Dawson states, Battersby believed she had a large fortune. Sarah Ann Stovin was underage and a ward of the court, and Battersby 'committed gross and wilful perjury' in obtaining a licence then used all of her funds to secure £160 which he borrowed from an attorney.

According to Dawson, Battersby's marriage to Sarah Ann was:

> '...consummated at a Brothel, and when the lady was not in the state of health to allow of such an act, but he declared she was his wife and he would do as he pleased.'

Battersby had 'diseased' his second wife too, a fact for which there was medical corroboration. Dawson describes Sarah Ann Stovin as:

> 'a weak person whose education has been much neglected, and … easily fell a prey to the wantonness and depravity of the Prisoner…'

The attorney who had lent Battersby money made efforts to recover the same through his second wife and through promises to help mitigate Batterby's sentence. However, this had been halted when the Mucklestons became involved.

Dawson expresses his surprise at some of the army personnel who gave Battersby a good character reference, and adds that Battersby's sister, Mrs Law of Sackville Street, Dublin, made it clear the family did not keep in contact with, nor support her brother.

Battersby was transported to Sydney, New South Wales, on the *Portsea* in July 1838 and petitioned the Home Secretary from there. He claims never to have received any money from Ann Muckleston and that he 'lived in terms of perfect cordiality with his second wife from the day of their marriage up to the time of his conviction.' He declares he has not received any portion of property from Sarah Ann Stovin.

Battersby's actions gave Ann Muckleston grounds for divorce which she was granted in 1840.[3] Between 1801 and 1850, only four women obtained a parliamentary divorce based on adultery. Grounds for a parliamentary divorce by a single act of adultery applied to a man divorcing his wife; a woman divorcing her husband needed to prove he was guilty of additional offences. According to Roderick Phillips in his book, *Untying the Knot: A short history of Divorce*,[4] Ann was one of only two women who obtained it based on adultery aggravated by bigamy, whilst the other two cases were based on incestuous adultery between the husband and wife's sister.

New South Wales Archives show Arthur Battersby/Napier Disney received a Certificate of Freedom on 29 January 1845.

Elizabeth Wood Lloyd (or **Loyd**) enjoyed several identities. On the morning of 2 May 1814, at the age of 16, Elizabeth Wood Ducket, spinster, was married to Thomas Lloyd (or Loyd), bachelor, by the Reverend H. Chapman at St Mary le bone, London. On 28 May 1822, Elizabeth married again, this time under the name of Betty Wood Louther (or Lowther) Blythe (or Bligh or Blyth), a widow. Her new husband was William Henry Truss, bachelor, and the wedding had taken place at their parish church, St Pancras, also in London. The ceremony was conducted by William Tullfield, in the presence of Octavious Young Thistleton and G. Hamp. Almost four years after Elizabeth married William Truss, she was sentenced to seven years transportation, having been found guilty of bigamy at the Old Bailey, April Sessions, 1826. The prosecutor was Truss; Thomas Lloyd was still alive.

An arrest warrant was served on Elizabeth and she was brought before the magistrates at the Hatton Garden Police Office, on 13 March 1826. Reports of the arrest and subsequent hearing were carried by newspapers including the *Globe* and *The Times*, the latter relating how the case had taken up much court time and had aroused a great deal of interest. Perhaps to stoke that interest, Elizabeth was described as wearing the latest fashions, her face hidden behind a dark veil, whilst, allegedly, she appeared unconcerned throughout.

The prosecution could not produce the two witnesses to Elizabeth's first marriage. The first, her father, had since died and the second, a female who also served as a bridesmaid, was now living too far away to appear. However, Truss's attorney was certain the writing on the marriage certificates belonged to her and other witnesses were brought forward who confirmed she had always called Lloyd her husband, although she had since told one witness that Lloyd had died some time ago.

At the hearing, William Truss, who worked in the Auditor's Office, East India House, claimed Elizabeth had called herself the widow of Captain Blyth since he first met her a few years before. It was only when he discovered she had recently been unfaithful and he had asked his solicitor to draw up a deed of separation affording her an allowance, that he found out that she had been untruthful regarding her marital status.

Elizabeth was committed to Newgate for trial. The description of her in the Newgate Register of Prisoners is more basic in its detail than the newspaper reports of the Hatton Garden hearing; 5ft 3in in height, 'fresh' in complexion, with brown hair and grey eyes. Her stature is given as 'stout'.

At Elizabeth's trial at the Old Bailey April Sessions,[5] the prosecution quickly established that her marriage to Thomas Lloyd had taken place. William Parr, the clerk and registrar of marriages at St Mary Le Bone, confirmed that he had the register. Robert Blackmore, William Truss's attorney, swore that the handwriting in the register belonged to Elizabeth, as did Mr and Mrs Yates, above whom she had lived with Blyth, although the Yates both agreed that her handwriting had since improved. Other witnesses, including Mary Ann Pearson, a one-time lodger in Elizabeth's family house, now living at North Place, Back Road, Islington and David Jackson, a neighbour of the Duckets, confirmed she had told them that she had married Lloyd, as they had when they appeared as witnesses at the Hatton Garden hearing.

The court heard more details of Elizabeth's life in the years between her marriages to Lloyd and to Truss, which lead to a guilty verdict and a sentence of seven years transportation. But details within her petition to the Home Secretary, Robert Peel, provide a fuller picture of those intervening years.

Elizabeth was still only 26 (or 28 according to the Old Bailey Proceedings and Newgate Register) when she petitioned the Home Secretary for mercy. She began with 'A Brief statement of circumstances relative to the situation and conduct of Mrs Loyd…' but the 'brief statement' is six pages long. She claimed that she did not know that Thomas Lloyd was still alive and, that aside, had thought the marriage had been legally ended after she had been sold to Blyth for five shillings, which was a mutually agreeable separation arrangement. Moreover, having taken legal advice from a solicitor friend, she had no reason to assume she had done anything wrong. She had not deceived Truss, to whom she had told her history and he had been keen to marry her. When they had separated, he had promised to pay her £120 per annum, but the money had not been forthcoming. Supplementing the 'brief statement of circumstances …' was a second document giving Elizabeth's version of her life.

She was the daughter of George Ducket, and was born in Carlisle, in Cumberland. The family lived in John Street, Marylebone and at around the age of 16 she was courted by Thomas Lloyd, a baker. On the morning of 2 May 1814, the couple married, she being 'furnished with every necessary for such occasion' by her father. But her father died later that same month following a short illness and Elizabeth 'at so tender age was cast upon the world without the affectionate advice of a best friend ...' It was to her new husband Lloyd then that she looked for protection.

Although the couple first lived in Elizabeth's father's house, she claimed that once her father was buried, her husband insisted she left that house immediately and he found them an apartment in the house of a friend. Although Elizabeth doesn't give an address, it seems this, or their next address, was in Rathbone Place, according to Thomas Stevens, witness and fellow baker, at her Old Bailey trial. But according to Elizabeth, the marriage had its problems. Not long after the couple moved, Lloyd sent in a broker and sold all the furniture. She was pregnant at the time with her first child, so Lloyd then took a furnished lodging and Elizabeth continued to work as a dressmaker. However, Lloyd drank away all the couple's earnings, meaning she suffered 'the severest privations' during the later stages of her pregnancy, with 'not a morsel of Bread or even anything in the House to support nature...' After a fortnight, she could bear it no longer and went to her mother's house with the child. At this time, she was also wet-nursing another child for which she received half a guinea a week, and it was the 'great kindness' of those associated with this child that ensured she had essentials. But Lloyd 'prevailed on her' and she returned to him.

Elizabeth continued to work 'at her needle' and had employment in Princess Street, Hanover Square; furnished lodgings were again provided, but Lloyd continued to drink, spending all her earnings, often fifteen shillings a week, and using her 'very ill at all times' when she returned home from work.

Now pregnant with her second child, Elizabeth continued to work, but arriving home one day, she found Lloyd had pledged the sheets from their bed. To avert any prosecution for stealing from their lodgings, she had no option but to redeem them. It was not surprising, then, she felt 'compelled' to leave Lloyd. It was 1816 and Elizabeth claimed she didn't see Lloyd again from the end of March until her brother came home from sea on 31 May of the same year.

Elizabeth told the Home Secretary that her brother had been away for seven years, serving on a man-of-war. Now back, he learnt of her situation and he and Elizabeth's mother decided to ask Lloyd to part from Elizabeth. With her brother leading negotiations, Lloyd eventually agreed to sell her if they paid him five shillings. Elizabeth's mother sought legal advice, at the cost of two guineas, and the solicitor advised that Elizabeth would be 'as free as before she was married to Lloyd' providing the sale was made, and as long as the purchaser was not a relative. In addition, the purchaser's name had to be 'taken care of'. Elizabeth's brother knew a fellow sailor who had returned with him from sea, and this young man agreed to buy her, 'although', Elizabeth wrote, 'with no other intention than to free her from her husband'. Lloyd agreed never to 'molest or hinder' her in any way and on 5 June 1816 Elizabeth was sold to the young man whose name was '– Blyth'.

According to Elizabeth, the agreement was passed to Mr Humphries, her solicitor, for her trial at the Old Bailey, but 'it is very much to be regretted that the same was held back on so important an occasion' otherwise she would not, she believed, 'be labouring under so severe and dreadful a sentence as that of transportation for seven years.' She acknowledged that agreeing to this type of separation, and taking Blyth's name, might lead to assumptions about her character but, Elizabeth emphasised, she:

> 'consented <u>only and solely</u> for the purpose of obtaining a separation … and was not proposing or in any way to have in view improper purposes.'

She insisted the child she was carrying was Lloyd's and was named after Blyth 'merely in accordance with his desire, as complimentary.'

Witnesses at the Old Bailey gave a different account of the sale of Elizabeth to Blyth, who John Yates named as 'George Bligh'. Thomas Stevens, stated that he had known Elizabeth fifteen years and had been a lodger in her mother's house; Thomas Lloyd had been a god-father to one of his children. He remembered Elizabeth and Lloyd marrying around the time of the annual Yorkshire Stingo fair, held every May in Lisson Green, Marylebone, based around the pub of the same name. The last time he saw the couple together was about ten years ago when he, Lloyd, Elizabeth and Blyth were drinking together. Elizabeth was on Blyth's knee and the group ordered a half a pint of gin. According to Stevens, Lloyd then said to Elizabeth that if she preferred Blyth to him, then she should go with him. Blyth tossed five shillings onto the table and left with Elizabeth while Stevens and Lloyd stayed drinking the gin. On cross-examination, Stevens confirmed the money was provided by Blyth but when asked if Lloyd picked it up, replied the landlord did. Although he doesn't explain why the landlord did this, it is possible it was to pay for the gin.

Elizabeth's petitions claimed she carried on with her dress-making 'in a comfortable way' to support herself and was respected by upright families and individuals. She did not see Lloyd again until she met him in Hatton Garden Police Office after her arrest: she did not know he was 'in existence'.

Details of Elizabeth's life with Blyth come from Old Bailey witness John Yates, a cooper. About October 1822, Elizabeth had rented an apartment from Yates, lodging with him for around a week. She used the name Blyth ('Bligh') and George was with her. The next year the couple came again and stayed for two to three weeks following Blyth's trip to the East Indies. The year after that, Elizabeth returned, still using the name Blyth. Mrs Yates confirmed Blyth worked as a mate on an East India boat and seemed respectable; John Yates believed, from information Elizabeth gave him, that following George Blyth's return to sea the first time, she had become a companion to a lady who was deranged. The lady's name was Truss and she lived in Claremont Place. Yates told the Court he did not know whether or not Elizabeth resided with the woman but had been told by Elizabeth she was going back to her.

The meeting and subsequent marriage of Truss and Elizabeth are recounted in different ways by each party. Elizabeth wrote that on 29 May 1819 she was on her way home from a trip to Surrey, 'with a bunch of lilacs in her hand', when she was followed through Hatton Garden by William Truss. He 'importuned her as to having been for a walk' and when she didn't answer him 'he contrived the same importunity'. Eventually she told him to leave her fearing for her reputation, because 'her character was her support and she earned a livelihood by work'. Instead of going away, Truss gave her a present; and to get rid of him, she gave him a false address. However, he tracked her down and she received 'a letter expressive of anger at having a fictitious address given'. Truss threatened to come to her house if she did not meet with him and not wanting him to do so she met him to explain and to ask him to stop contacting her. But Truss carried on writing, continuing even when he went to Margate in August where he invited her to join him; she declined. At this time, she was suffering from an inflammation to the side of her face, due to 'closely attending her work'. She took a room at five shillings a week, still using the name Blyth even though she had not seen him for two years. She states she made enquiries about her first husband but was told he was dead. Details of those enquiries are not given.

At William Truss's instigation, another apartment was taken for her at twelve shillings per week, and because she was not extravagant she:

> '... argued upon the expensiveness of it and that of Mr Truss's own Apartments as he was also paying a guinea per week. [She told him] she would not continue with him at so expensive a rate ...'

Truss then suggested furnishing two rooms and a kitchen at an acceptable rate. They both lived there, in the Polygon, Sommers Town, 'a length of time' at a rent of £30 per year. Elizabeth claimed she was always frugal whilst 'under his protection' and 'was never absent from his house but in his company and that of meeting him to walk home as he came from London.' He kept proposing marriage to her until, she finally consented.

Elizabeth told the Home Secretary that Truss was fully aware of 'every particular of her former situation' and 'fully aware of all the particulars of her life, and that he cannot plead deception…' When married, they took a house in Claremont Place, Pentonville, but in less than three months his manner towards her had altered and she found his conduct intolerable. She fell out with some of his friends, and her attempts failed when she tried to reconcile the differences between her and her husband. Blaming Truss's friends' 'persuasions and malice', Elizabeth states that the couple separated. In early summer 1825, Truss consented to 'a separation and a division of the furniture' and agreed Elizabeth should live where she liked. She went to the house several times afterwards and Truss's 'brother', in London from Reading, insisted she should have a separate maintenance. Both parties were of the same opinion and an agreement was entered into on 28 December 1825 which provided her with £120 per annum and forbade either of them from harassing the other. However, no maintenance was forthcoming and Elizabeth was charged before a solicitor could act in her defence. No further mention is made of her children by her previous associations.

At the Old Bailey, William Henry Truss told the court he had not brought the prosecution only to invalidate the marriage; he had not taken it to Doctors' Commons. He knew Elizabeth as 'Betty Wood Louther Bligh' and, not knowing a Captain Bligh, he had no reason to doubt her when she said she was his widow. She told him she was well connected to the Lonsdale family, that Lady Styles and Mr Bosanquet were her mother's relatives, and talked of a rich aunt of the name of Hearn. When he took the witness stand, Truss's brother-in-law, John Aquila Brown, went further, saying Elizabeth had said she was the niece to Lady Styles. Truss had first met Elizabeth in the street, but she had always displayed proper conduct before they were married and, when asked, he confirmed he'd never paid her any money. They lived together for two years before they were married at St Pancras Old Church on 28 May 1822 and were together for four years afterwards. Truss said that Elizabeth had pressed him to marry her; he had not proposed it.

At first, they lived in Chalton Street, before moving to the Polygon in Sommers Town. Although the first two years went smoothly, this didn't last. At some point in their marriage – and perhaps before – contrary to Elizabeth's statement to the Home Secretary, Truss said Elizabeth often went away on visits. After they married, Captain Atkinson made several visits to their house and Truss believed him to be the trustee for Elizabeth's settlement, and the commander of a schooner, *St Helena*. The couple parted in December 1825; Truss agreed to allow her £120 per annum, still unaware Elizabeth had not told him the full facts of her past life.

John Aquila Brown, Truss's brother-in-law and a silversmith, gave evidence in court, saying he met Elizabeth ten days after the wedding. Roughly four weeks before the trial, he went with a police officer to Bognor, Sussex. There he and officer William Brown Edwards found Elizabeth in bed with Captain Atkinson. The group came back to London, with Elizabeth openly saying she had married Lloyd who had then sold her on to Blyth for a bottle of wine and five shillings.

Letter were produced in the court showing Elizabeth signing herself as Elizabeth Lloyd in 1816 and E.W. Truss in 1822. A 'guilty' verdict was passed.

Elizabeth's petition, sent from Newgate prison to Robert Peel on 1 May 1826, was unsuccessful, despite attaching the signatures of fifty supporters attesting to her previous good conduct. Her claim for 'illegal advice being given by a solicitor as to the validity of the first separation by a Sale of the Deponent' held no sway. Nor did her statement that no burden of family had been left upon either party in regard to William Truss and he had 'full knowledge of all the circumstances (laying aside deception).'

The *Examiner*, 'A Sunday Paper, on Politics, Domestic Economy, and Theatricals', for the year 1826; reported on Elizabeth's case, telling how she had misrepresented herself to Truss, calling herself the widow of 'Captain Bligh' and falsely claiming high connections. However, its account carried an error; it suggested she had married Lloyd since her separation from Truss and whilst Truss, 'a clerk in the India House' was still living, rather than the other way around.

According to the Newgate Register, Elizabeth was kept in Newgate prison until 15 August 1826, then was sent on the *Sir Charles Forbes* to Van Diemen's Land, arriving in January 1827.

Upon arrival in Van Diemen's Land, Tasmanian Archives show she stated her husband was 'first clerk in the Auditors Office, £800 year' and gave his name as William Truss, adding she had thought her first husband was dead.

But on 16 March 1829, Elizabeth's name was in the conduct book, having been found in the house of 'one Mark Hillas' at half past ten in the evening.

By 17 December of the same year she was in the conduct book again being 'Repeatedly absent without leave but particularly the whole of last night'. By 27 March 1833, her conduct had not improved. The book noted that she held a general pass but had displayed 'Disorderly, immoral and disgraceful conduct.' She was removed to the 3rd class Female Factory, (House of Correction), Hobart Town, for the remainder of her original sentence.

Elizabeth was given permission to marry on two occasions, the first to James Westwood on 31 August 1832 and the second to Henry Douglass. James Westwood was a fellow convict who had been transported on the *Caledonia*, arriving in 1820. He was a tin plate worker or carpenter, 23 years old at the time of arrival according to the convicts' register, who had been convicted of burglary at Worcestershire Assizes where he received a sentence of fourteen years. He was 5ft 5½in tall, with black hair, light blue eyes and a propensity to get in to trouble. There seems to be no record of the marriage taking place, but despite his early record of bad behaviour, Westwood received a Conditional Pardon in 1835 and a Free Certificate two years later.

Elizabeth married Henry Douglass on 29 October 1834. In their marriage registration, Henry is described as a bachelor and Elizabeth, always now seemingly calling herself Elizabeth Wood Lloyd, is described as a widow. Both are residents of Launceston, County of Cornwall, Van Diemen's Land. Their marriage was conducted by John Anderson, 'minister of the Scotch church', and witnessed by Richard Evans and Elizabeth Steel.

Just over four years later, on 13 January 1839, Elizabeth died.[6] Her death was registered under the name of Elizabeth Wood Douglas on 17 January 1839 by John Bryant, the Hobart Town Sexton. The cause of death appears to be 'Decline'.

Chapter 3

Words from the Hulks

In the final decades of the eighteenth century, the hulks had been introduced as a temporary solution to alleviate overcrowded prisons. With transportation to America no longer an option and those awaiting transportation to Australia exceeding the number of places on transportation ships, many prisoners were sent to the prison hulks, themselves full to overflowing. Varying in size and type, the hulks included old war ships and former trading vessels adapted as floating prisons and moored off the English coast, as well as off Gibraltar and Bermuda. (See Appendix 2).

Prisoners' stays on the hulks varied from weeks to years, depending upon the timing of their arrival there, the prisoners' physical and mental suitability for transportation, and the departure dates of transportation ships to New South Wales or Van Diemen's Land. Many served out their sentence on the hulks, never leaving home waters, whilst others were released early, beneficiaries of the Overseer or Captain's Quarterly Recommendation Lists which put forward a number of prisoners for early release. The criteria for these lists were usually fixed; e.g. only those prisoners who had served more than half of their sentence could be considered, and they had to be amongst the best behaved of those with whom they were imprisoned. A strict percentage of names could be suggested and a maximum of two thirds of the most deserving would be approved. The lists were often annotated with muster reports or details of exceptional behaviour. Although not all those recommended were released, enough spaces were created to accommodate new prisoners who would endure the same process.

The September 1832 Recommendation list for the *Cumberland* hulk[1] at Chatham shows that three out of every 100 prisoners were put forward, twenty-four names in total. Prisoner 2881 in the ship's book, **William Blackman**, had his recommendation approved despite being a repeat offender. Aged thirty, he had been convicted of larceny at the Old Bailey in February 1828. Of his original seven year sentence, he had served four years, seven months and nine days. His gaol report stated 'Here before' but on the quarterly muster he had received 'G' (good) seven times and 'VG' (very good) eleven times. The annotation against his name notes, 'This man has been very useful as a Plumber on numerous occasions on board the Hulks at this place.'

However, 24-year-old **James Beresford**, (Number 2208) was unsuccessful on this occasion. He had been convicted at Worcester Assizes in March 1827, guilty of stealing geese. At the time of the recommendation, he had served five years, six months and twenty days of a seven year sentence. His gaol report stated 'Not known before' and his behaviour in gaol had been good. On the hulk quarterly muster he received eight 'Goods', eleven 'Very goods' and one 'Very bad'. The reason for his rejection appears to be found in the annotation; he had prevented the escape of two prisoners whilst he was a gangsman, but when he was a cook in the 'Gallery Forward' he was connected with others stealing and concealing a quantity of beef.

Men and boys were mixed on hulks until around 1824, when men were removed from the *Bellerophon*, thus creating the first hulk for boy prisoners. Around two years later the boys were moved to the more suitable *Euryalus*. Although women were not generally sent to the hulks, some were moved there as a temporary measure when the Penitentiary at Millbank experienced an epidemic in 1823. The 15 May 1824 Recommendation List for the *Narcissus* and *Heroine* puts forward the names of twenty-six women.[2] The covering letter states the thirteen women from the *Heroine* are all those remaining on board. The Home Office annotation shows free pardons were granted later that month and that the then Home Secretary, Robert Peel, hoped this would help 'the Committee' release one of the ships.

Convicts left the hulks in the day time to work on shore or in the dock yards, where their labour was put to use in skilled or unskilled ways such as carpentry, road building and construction. In Bermuda, under punishing climatic conditions, prisoner labour was used in the building of the Royal Naval Dockyard, with the hulks serving as their prison accommodation.

On board the hulks, physical and mental conditions were arduous for the shackled prisoners and the hulks' miserable reputation spread before them. Letters from prisoners, within the Home Office petitions, give details of the personal trials and hardship.

In April 1821, **William Higham** wrote to his friend Henry Willoughby from the transport ship *Countess of Harcourt* which was about to sail to Van Diemen's Land. Henry Willoughby was a prisoner on the *Bellerophon* hulk at Sheerness, as Higham had been. On the back of the folded letter, Higham has written 'we sail on Sunday' and his feelings on leaving the hulks is clear. 28-year-old Higham had been tried at the Old Bailey, September 1820 and found guilty of stealing but 'not guilty' of the charge of burglary. He received a sentence of seven years transportation.

Higham begins by saying that he is writing as promised and he hopes:

'... will find you As well And I wish you As comfortable as I ham But that I No you neavous Can Be while you are on that oppressive Arbitrary Miserable hulk Thanks Be to God that I ham Delivered from that Den of Lions & ham happy to enform you that we Are now treated like Christians Not like thieves We have no half hanged poverty struck guards to take Every mean Dirty Advantage of us that offered itself to their Notise Neather have we Any Good Man of the House to condemn us to Hell weather or No Can he tell the inside of A Man Does he No a mans Heart Why Are we to Stand Before The good man of your house to Be Abused And told you must come to school Does A man whant to Become 3 times A child But I have something to say that the good man of your house is to Blind that he cannot see the policy that A general part of his flock Are Hypocrites... the mode he takes to force men in to that Chapel whare they Dam in thairs hearts what they would otherwise old sacret a hulk of corruption a school for Scandal ...'

Appearing to write about beatings and informers, (which Higham refers to as 'Noses') he continues:

'... if wa was to send us All the noses you Have in your Ship we could Blood soon cuer them Even Mr Coursons we make it a [illegible] them old Honester and Higgans I think will never turn Noses Again I wish we had a few more of them here for I ham sure the physick we do minister to them wood soon have its desired Affects upon them we have had several good fights tell Clark we Cross [train them] in good Form And that old tom martn gives us his swig swig sway And scattering Bag in fine stile we deal in wooley chan And winde gleesers And I do All our Business in the Regular way of Dealing...'

Higham ends by adding:

'I ham glad to hear Crag As got his Liberty My Best Respectts to All enquiring Frends and Believe me your Ever Sincere frend And Well wishes, Wm Higham'.

William Higham arrived in Van Diemen's Land in July 1821 but his seems not to have been a story of new beginnings. According to Tasmanian Archives, after years of bad conduct, William Higham was found guilty of 'bushrangling and robbery' and executed on 5 January 1833.

At the Old Bailey December Sessions 1823, **William Hay**, also known as **James Hay**, was found guilty of uttering a forged £5 note. (See also Chapter 6). He was sentenced to death but his case was considered at King in Council on 19 March 1824 and reduced to transportation for life.

On 6 May 1824, the day after his arrival on board the *York* hulk at Gosport, Hay wrote to his father's one time solicitor, and his sole supporter, John Bennell, to tell him that he has 'savely' arrived on the hulk and to use Hay's number (4531) and both names when writing to him. Hay expresses his desire to leave the country in preference to spending 'about 6 years' on the hulk and continues:

> 'As I tend greatly in need of a Box and there is one to dispose here for about 5/- my leaving Newgate so unexpectedly I had nothing remaining and if you will send your Clerk to Mr Beckett's Bell, Church End, Houndsditch most likely they may have a trifle or something for me… A little ready money is absolutely required and in fact cannot be done without when persons first arrive on board.'

Hay was in Newgate prison at the same time as William Henry Reynolds (see Chapter 8) and met him there or in their mutual parish of St Botolph's. He asks Bennell if he would be kind enough to send his Clerk to Newgate 'and tell William H Reynolds that I send my best respects and am arrived save on board the Vessell'.

Although several petitions to the Home Office claim ill treatment of the prisoner with over- zealous punishment, as did **William Burgess** on the *Justitia* hulk in the same year as Hay arrived on board the *York*, Hay writes of a relative kindness:

> 'After my arrival at this place of destination a Gentleman, Mr Bailey, the chief officer or Mate had the infinite goodness to direct that I should only have a small iron on my left leg on account of my right being lame and having the scars of disease I was afflicted with about 12 or 14 years back.'

Maintaining order on board was undoubtedly a constant balancing of punishment and deterrent with small humanities.

Describing his initial impressions of the atmosphere, Hay writes:

'There is a very pleasant prospect around as when on deck but rather terrific and gloomy in the wards we are placed which cannot but increase and depress rather than cheer the spirits of the foolish misguided unfortunate persons who resign their liberty and comfortable homes to dwell in the wretched confins of slavery, Oh God! could I have dreamt or even pictured the outlines of what undoubtedly must be the merited rewards for those who dare to infringe upon the laws of God...'

He adds as a PS at the end of his letter:

'I have nothing to pay any postage with or assist myself.'

Two weeks later, on 20 May 1824, Hay wrote to Bennell again and his spirits are lower. He explains that he is taking the opportunity of sending this letter via a prisoner's friend, who has been to the hulk and is returning, because:

'I have written twice before but have strong grounds to fully believe that they have never been sent as it is a very customary thing in the Ship but one I got out by the Prisoner whose friend will carry this.'

Of the *York* he writes:

'This place of confinement is ~~horror~~ [sic] direful and miserable to extreme for there is all manner of device practiced.'

Later in the letter he returns to the conditions:

'I am truly miserable here for this a hell upon earth for the work is too hard and the food wretchedly miserable and not fit to give pigs for there is some semblance when it is served out for every one eats out of one mess. If you received my last letter you will be able to judge. I have time left 5 o'clock in the morning and going to work till 12 on a pint of boiled barley and nothing with it.'

On 2 July 1824, Hay wrote to Bennell once more not having received 'even so trifling' assistance from him.

'My present situation is in every degree worse than can in general be even supposed for the food is not only hardly a subsistence but the society is invariably of the extremely lowest Class bordering on the brute creations at good, conduct and uniform language of terrific expressions. In fact the infinite misery I have to endure now is surpassing the feelings of a susceptible mind and Newgate in every sense was a paradise in comparison to this. The terror of the sufferings I shall have to undergo should I have to remain here during the winter, with the privation of food and no fire to go to when cold or wet with the inclemency of the weather stimulates me for this sanguine <u>wish to go to some of the Colonies where no doubt I shall be</u> soon far better off than most probable I ever was or shall be in the future was I to remain in this Country after having lost my Character in London which being the centre of my profession. I wrote to the Captain (Lamb) of the hulk about my going in the 1st ship; he sanctioned my request and agreed with my reasons and said Mr Peel had been applied too and I should be sent of with the number of Prisoners ordered to be sent. however it is supposed that another Ship will come about the 20th Inst & if I am called upon if the Doctor passes me I shall go but not otherwise.' Hay asks Bennell again to try and get him some 'assistance', 'If not what clothes you kindly gave me and those I purchased I must sell for to buy myself some absolutely craving necessary food to stop the demands of my appetite & support me to work which I am forced to do beyond my regular strength and what my trade ever accustomed me.'

Hay tells Bennell that he is having to be 'circumspect in my detail' because 'men are flogged or punished for the most trifling things'. Referring to his current state, or perhaps to his former circumstances which ultimately lead to imprisonment (see Chapter 6):

'I have actually suffered already such agonised Grief and excrutiating pangs of hunger, that death would be a paradise ... I cannot picture the miseries of this place bad enough to convince you how really painful the tyranny is executed far too good for many characters and a great diel too cruel for others but there is no difference.'

Writing from on board the *Justitia* hulk at Woolwich in 1829, **William Strang** complained not about conditions but about being treated as a spectacle by his parents. He was a man of mixed interests: a surgeon, he was fond of prize-fighting and kept dubious company. Charged with theft of money and receipts he was taken in to Glasgow Gaol on 23 February 1829 and transmitted to Edinburgh on 15 May to stand trial at the High Court of Justiciary three days later. Found guilty, he was sentenced to transportation for seven years.

On 14 September 1829, his letter to his parents, possibly only a draft, first expressed sympathy for their lack of work and his mother's bad knee, but he continues:

'...I am very much surprised that you never come to see me but you bring somebody with you and it is as tho' I was to be made a show of, and if I have anything ever so particular to say to you I have no opportunity on account of some one or other with you, and I hope you will not take this amiss but I wish to be as strong as possible and to know no-one when I come home and as to Anne Loeg, she is quite a stranger to me for I don't remember seeing her these seven or eight years, so it cannot be any desire she can have of seeing me but only to see what sort of creature a Convict is, so when you come you can come by yourselves... and if there is anyone else with you when you come I shall not come down... and however I may appear at the time when they are a longside I really do not like the thoughts of being shewn as a kind of Monster...'

John Marcoux (or **Jean Babtiste Marcoux**) petitioned the Home Secretary twice; once, undated, from the *Racoon* hospital ship and once from on board the hulk *York* on 9 December 1835. Marcoux was a native of Lower Canada, 30 years old, married with two children and a jeweller by trade. He had purchased goods 'by the specious representations of David Le Fefre' who was convicted with him in Montreal, Lower Canada, March 1829. Guilty of sacrilege, though protesting his innocence, Marcoux was sentenced to death. The sentence had been commuted to transportation for life and he had been sent from 'the British Settlements of America' to Bermuda to complete the term. For almost five years he was employed in 'various mechanical branches for the use and benefit of the service' but his failing health lead to his transfer to England as an invalid, along with others in the same position. He had understood he would gain his freedom soon after.

He tells the Home Secretary:

'In the month of November 1833 we arrived in England and was placed on board the York Hulk Portsmouth from whence your petitioner was transfered to the Racoon Hospital ship. Health being partially restored, I was put in charge of the lunatics there on board the Hospital ship. Having devoted my time day and night to the objects in my charge, and for which Service, promises of the utmost importance were held out to me. I am constrained at length to throw myself on your Lordships consideration, the prisoners who came to England as invalids with your petitioner having all been liberated with the exception of your petitioner who is thousands of miles from his Native home, his wife and family having no friends to make intercession for him. Being entirely in a land of Strangers.'

Marcoux was suffering from 'Chronic affection of the Heart arising from Organic disease' according to the *Racoon*'s surgeon, Mr Williams. Despite Marcoux's claim of previous good conduct, the confirmation of such from Williams, Marcoux's concern his family 'are now cast on chance or the hand of charity for daily Bread in this wilderness world', his employability and offer to leave the country if freed, his petitions were marked 'Nil'.

On 16 July 1837 **Robert George** wrote to Thomas Wyatt, his brother in-law, from on board the hulk ship *Euryalus*. He was prompted to do so by a heightened awareness of being in England on borrowed time, knowing only the efforts of his commander has kept him from already being transported overseas. Unless his family and supporters could persuade the authorities to let him stay, and soon, his fate would be sealed and with it, any reasonable expectation of seeing his wife and children again.

Aged between 30 and 36,[3] Robert George, a carpenter from Tiverton, Devon, was working and living in London when he carried out the offence which led to his trial at the Old Bailey. In the August Sessions of 1835 he was convicted of 'Larceny in a Dwelling House', having stolen a silver pendant rod and small sextant on 18 July, items belonging to Edward Troughton. The Jury recommended mercy but the sentence of transportation for life was passed, reduced to seven years transportation on 28 September. (See also Chapter 4).

From Newgate, George was sent to the *Fortitude* hulk ship at Chatham, where, as prisoner number 2384, he used his carpentry skills as he would do also on the *Euryalus* hulk which sat alongside the *Fortitude*. Despite a petition being sent from family members, he felt he was facing an uncertain future when he wrote to Wyatt. He had previously heard the 'Establishment' was to be broken up and his removal would be inevitable. By 'Establishment' it would appear George means the hulk or the prisoners on it. Would this be his removal from England? The letter bears the mark 'Approved'

Beginning his letter 'Dear Friends' he writes:

> 'The reason I trouble you with thiss letter is to inform you that there is no order for me to be kept in this country and if there is not something done very shortly to that effect, I think the time is not far distant when I shall be call'd to go, in fact I should have been sent before thiss had it not been for the kindness of my commander who has kept me back for the express purpose to give you my friends an opportunity of doing something for me so that I might be detained in thiss country. I am Given to understand that Ld Palmerston will be with you shortly and then you will have an opportunity of speaking to him on my behalf has he promised you that I should not be sent out. I should thank you tell him that nothing but an order from the Secretary of the home department will effect it'

As with William Strang, Robert George had visitors and he writes that his wife, Sarah:

> '... was here about three months since and she informed me of the death of Mrs Pine and likewise of your continual illness of which I very much regret but I hope that you are recover'd and in perfect health.'

Interestingly he then addresses his parents, assuring them:

> '... the manner in which I am situated is very different in point of Comfort has it regards prisoners in general for the kindness that I received from the Commander and Officers of this Establishment is Great.'

It is not clear why he has received preferential treatment or whether this is true; possibly he is trying to allay his parents' fears.

Chapter 4

Theft

In a society yet to experience the full benefits of industrialisation, everyday commodities were still made by hand and of great value to their owners – and to thieves. Clothes, pots and pans, and metal were amongst goods stolen then sold on at markets, or pawned to raise cash by the many enduring impoverished and challenging conditions.

Crimes of theft were dealt with according to the value of the stolen articles, from where they were taken and how they were appropriated. Petitions received by the Home Office come from a wide range of offenders convicted of an equally wide range of thefts. Many seeking mercy were those found guilty of stealing animals in rural areas, or handkerchiefs and shoes in big cities where pickpocketing gangs were rife. 'Pickpocketing' had ceased to be a capital offence in 1808, but strong deterrents were still needed and were still meted out. The offence of 'Stealing from master' was created in 1823; it applied to any employee and was used for domestic servants as well as those workers outside the home as industrialisation grew.

Some youthful pick-pocketers received the maximum sentence of transportation for life, as was the case of 16-year-old Edward Norman, and his co-accused William Turner, when they appeared at the Old Bailey in 1825 accused of stealing a handkerchief.[1] Other convicted young pick-pocketers received a whipping then release or a short prison sentence, the latter being the punishment given to **John Wise**. He was 12 years old when he stole nuts from bags that had been knocked over in Covent Garden, in the spring of 1837. Unaware his son had been taken to the Station House, Wise's father had handbills printed and circulated, believing him to be missing. He was sentenced to two weeks in Westminster Bridewell and his father petitioned for his son's release, claiming the boy had previously been well behaved but had been led astray by an older child. However, the gaoler's report gave a different view. 'A bad boy. The beadles of the market complained.' Seemingly his sentence was not reduced and the Home Office annotation reads, 'Usual answer'.

When 19-year-old **Edward Rogers Faning** (or **Edward Roger Faning**) was convicted of theft at the Old Bailey[2] in January 1832, neither he nor his family were expecting the sentence of death which he received, especially as his father was the prosecutor.

Edward Rogers Faning was an apprentice law writer, the eldest of eight (or nine) children, in a respectable family. His father, Edward Faning senior, was an employee in the printing office of Messers Hansard, printers to the House of Commons, where he had worked since approximately 1815. But Faning junior fell into bad company and his behaviour towards his family was less than exemplary; not only was his conduct poor but he continually stole from his father. The last straw came on 18 December 1831 when Faning junior stole two coats, (worth £4 16s), two shawls (worth 15s) and one waistcoat, worth the same. His father, the victim, felt he had no option other than to prosecute.

Faning pleaded guilty before his parents arrived at the Session House and was sentenced to death. His ultimate fate now lay in the hands of the meeting of the King in Council.

Following the sentence, but before the case was considered in Council, Faning's father sent a petition to the Home Secretary to plead for a commutation of what he referred to as 'that dreadful event' on behalf of his son in Newgate prison. In his letter to Lord Melbourne dated 12 January 1832, Edward Faning explained how his son had come to be in this situation:

> 'Bad company, and bad advice (contrary to that of his parents) have been his ruin; but it is hoped that the education bestowed on the prisoner, and his youth (19th year), will plead with you in the recommending to his most gracious majesty a milder sentence.'

He suggested his son could still retrieve his character and become a useful member of society if he is sent to 'some of the colonies'.

Faning's case was considered at King in Council on 6 February 1832, along with prisoners whose crimes included horse-stealing, forgery and highway robbery. His death sentence was commuted to transportation for life and from Newgate prison, Faning junior was sent to the *Retribution* hulk at Sheerness.

His father wrote to the Home Secretary again, on behalf of himself and his wife Cordelia, who were then living at 48, Leather Lane, Holborn. His letter is undated but refers to his son's now commuted sentence and it betrays increasing anxiety. Both parents were in 'great distress of body and mind' and they 'most anxiously entreat your kind aid' in remitting part of the sentence. In an attempt to emphasise his son's remorse and shame he explained that he had:

'... persisted in pleading guilty, under a false impression that his punishment would not be so heavy, and likewise to avoid the severe affliction that it would occasion by seeing his parents (Your Petitioners) called on as prosecutors.'

However, by doing so, he had made his own position worse: his father explained, it prevented his son's supporters from making any application to the Court, should a jury have found him guilty.

To this letter, the Fanings appended a petition signed by forty-six supporters, many of whom were friends and neighbours living in Leather Lane and Eyre Street Hill, attesting to the respectable manner in which the Fanings had raised their son. The petition had no effect. In August 1832, Faning junior was sent from Sheerness to Ireland Island, Bermuda, to provide labour on the works. Whilst their son was on board the *Dromedary* hulk there, his parents did not stop petitioning.

On 18 June 1833, Edward Faning senior wrote to Lord Melbourne again, on behalf of himself and his wife, now living at 16 Myddleton Street, Spa Fields in London. This time he tried to explain his own guilt, turmoil and remorse at his actions which had caused his son, and presumably the rest of the family, such distress. He wrote of himself, 'who though willing to punish crime, would rather have forgone the prosecution than lived to bear the pangs which now afflict him by the bereavement of his eldest son.' He reiterated the respectable though humble manner in which his son was raised and explained again his only reason for bringing the prosecution was his hope of rescuing his son 'from mixing with a society of bad youths, encouraged by a party of low public-house keepers, some of whom are now suffering in prison from their bad conduct'. He emphasised Faning junior was penitent and he and his wife forgave him. Unfortunately, he did not receive news to assuage his guilt. The petition is marked 'Nil'.

In 1836, with Faning junior still in Bermuda, and the family still in Myddleton Street, Spa Fields, Edward Faning again petitioned Lord Melbourne. He quoted an extract from a communication he'd received from his son in which he had expressed 'his heartfelt contrition' and further quoted:

'"I can assure you if you should prove fortunate enough to get my sentence mitigated, I shall repay all my past bad conduct by proving myself a dutiful son, and by doing all that lies in my power to render your old age comfortable; and I assure you that I have long ere this seen my folly, and heartily repented of all my base actions and ingratitude to you.'"

Edward Faning senior once more stated he had prosecuted:

'in order that his son might be deterred from following a vicious course of life which he was led in to by a dissolute set of companions he had fallen in with.'

He believed his son's conduct since his conviction was good, and Captain Hire of the *Dromedary* had no bad reports against him. The letter was undersigned by thirty-five supporters, including Luke Hansard, James Hansard and Luke Hansard junior, for whom Faning senior was still working as an overseer, but this did not lead to a commutation of sentence by the Home Office. The petition was marked 'Nil' and a reply to that effect was sent on 1 July 1836. This petition has been annotated by one of the Home Office clerks as a note to aid the Home Secretary's decision. It shows the prisoner's conduct on board the *Dromedary* as '1 muster bad, 2 musters indifferent, the rest good'.

Faning junior returned from Bermuda to England in October 1840 and became a prisoner on the hulks at Portsmouth. When his father knew his son had been sent back to England, he prepared the younger siblings' minds 'to receive their long lost brother'. This he told the Home Secretary in his petition of November 1841 and reminded him Faning junior had endured ten years of punishment. To help his son's case, he had arranged 'a situation' for the prisoner as a law clerk, through the medium of William S. Jump, cashier clerk to Smithson and Milton, 23 Southampton Buildings, Chancery Lane, Solicitors; a letter from Swayne Jump to that effect was forwarded to the Home Office. Faning senior's letter has been annotated, 'liberate' and Edward Rogers Faning received a free pardon on 20 November 1841.

Prisoner **Robert George** wrote to his family from the hulks as shown in Chapter 3. The details of the offence which lead to him being there are as follows. George, was working as a carpenter in London when he stole a silver pendant rod and small sextant belonging to the late Edward Troughton on 18 July 1835. Troughton had died and Robert George had been employed to work at his property where he succumbed to temptation. George was prosecuted by Troughton's executor, William Simms (or Symms) of Fleet Street, an optician, who had known George for several years. He stood trial at the Old Bailey, August Sessions, where he was convicted of larceny in a specific place, a dwelling house.

According to the report in Old Bailey Proceedings,[3] Robert George had tried to sell the silver rod to the shop of Kneller Smart in Princes Street, Leicester Square. The assistant, Thomas Farrant, gave evidence stating that when the shop owner asked George where he had obtained it and if he could supply the other part, George had given them a false name and address. He'd told them he'd found it in the toilet of an empty house and a fellow brick-layer had the other piece. Farrant made enquiries and tracked George to his home, whereupon he saw Mrs George and the sextant.

There was discussion at the trial regarding the value of the stolen items, but it was agreed they totalled more than £5. Robert George was found guilty. The prosecutor recommended mercy but the sentence of transportation for life was passed.

A few weeks later, on 28 September, George's sentence was reduced to seven years transportation. Robert George was not a hardened criminal. At his trial, reasons for clemency centred on his previous exemplary character before this, his first offence, and character witnesses attested to that fact. William Simms stated that George had earlier opportunities to steal items of greater value than those he had taken that July, but had not before been tempted. Petitions to the Home Office state he had an 'upstanding' wife and four children to support, the eldest eight years old and the youngest two or three months. At the time he committed the crime however, domestic difficulties had put economic pressures upon him and the recent death of another of his children led to expenses he might have found difficult to meet.

Robert George's family and friends began petitioning for him to be allowed to stay in England by seeking the support of Viscount Palmerston, then Foreign Secretary, and Lord John Russell, Home Secretary. George's wife, Sarah, living at Little Wild Street, Lincoln's Inn Fields, London, sent at least two petitions. The first was undersigned by fifteen supporters including William Simms and George's former employer John Barron. The second was undersigned by twenty-three supporters, including Simms, who also sent a separate petition. George's mother-in-law Sarah Whyatt became involved as did Christopher Woollacott, of the Little Wild Street Baptist Church. Certificates of good behaviour on the hulks were forwarded. Robert George himself petitioned twice

On board the hulks, Robert George maintained his good reputation, and character references submitted throughout his incarceration include those from Henry George Dawes, chaplain of St Margarets, Rochester, Kent and the *Euryalus*, and from Thomas Hubburd, the prisoner's master on board the same. George received a free pardon 1 August 1839.

Like Robert George, **William Strang** had written a letter from the hulk, as shown in Chapter 3. He too had been found guilty of theft but his initial sentence was transportation for seven years and the details of his offence are very different from that committed by George.

Strang petitioned the king from the Tolbooth in Edinburgh, and claimed this was his first offence, 'committed by opening a chest in a shop in Glasgow and by carrying off a small sum of money and certain deposit Receipts'. He stated he wasn't the perpetrator of the crime but confessed his shame at being concerned in this 'disgraceful transaction'. His fondness for prize-fighting had led to his involvement with acquaintances he described as being 'far below his proper sphere in life'. Needing money, he was 'seduced to share in this Solitary instance in the unhallowed gains of his new associates.'

Strang outlined his qualifications. He had received a 'Liberal Education' and quickly gained a Diploma as a Surgeon. He stated the public prosecutor at his trial acknowledged his previous character had been unblemished. His behaviour in jail, he claimed, 'has been most exemplary' and his was not a case of an ordinary convict or of one hardened by crime. He was anxious to maintain his suitability for employment and wanted to continue his studies; if his sentence could not be mitigated, he asked if he could be employed giving medical assistance either at the Penitentiary or to the Convicts 'by regular or occasional attendance in such manner as may be most suitable and proper.'

Strang's credentials were confirmed in a letter from D. Macfarlain, James Millar and John McLaurin, Minister, sent from Glasgow College on 23 June 1829. He had studied there for four years, focusing mostly on Anatomy and Surgery for which he had shown a talent. The letter writers stated that his skills could be put to good use even if that use was 'in a quarter of the Globe remote from his early connections and unfortunate Associations'. They too claimed this was Strang's first offence and his father was of a good character.

Strang's good conduct whilst imprisoned was confirmed in a letter of early June from Dugald McColl, Governor of Glasgow Gaol; the Chaplain, John Fisher, concurred. Others supported him whilst he was imprisoned. On 29 June 1829, a petition was sent from sixteen neighbours in Glasgow, and James Christie, Commissioner of Police. The reasons they gave were that Strang was 'an only son and as his worthy and indulgent father has spared no cost to render him a useful and dignified member of society'. On 30 June 1829, a supportive character reference had been sent from William D Scott, LLD, 'private lecturer in Philosophy and teacher of languages' in Glasgow.

Strang had studied under him for 'upwards of four years' and Scott did not stint in his praise for his student, noting that throughout that time:

> 'the whole bent of his mind seemed solely directed to the cultivation of learning that he uniformly evinced a genius above common and such propriety of character and conduct as justly merited the most unequivocal commendations.'

On 6 July 1829, a supportive petition was sent from sixteen local people and the following day George Salmond, the Procurator Fiscal of Lanarkshire, wrote from the Sheriff's chambers confirming Strang was not known to them before this offence. The same was confirmed by the Procurator Fiscal of Glasgow.

At first, Robert Peel, the Home Secretary, decided to send Strang to the General Penitentiary in London. An annotation on the back of a letter from the Earl of Glasgow, sent on 9 July states, 'Let him go to the Penitentiary, but just as any other convict [illegible] there'. The decision was relayed to the Earl of Glasgow on 18 July and in turn the Earl of Glasgow sent the information to Strang's father. The Home Office gave the same information to Archibald Campbell MP, Lord Lieutenant of Renfrewshire, who had forwarded a supporting petition from five people on 17 July. With the decision seemingly made, Strang's father started planning for his son to be supplied with 'a pair of shoes which in all probability he will require as well as any other little article …' he would need at Millbank. But the situation soon changed.

Writing to the Earl of Glasgow on 23 July 1829, Robert Peel told of a development in Strang's situation since their previous correspondence less than a week earlier. A report on the prisoners under sentence of transportation in Edinburgh gaol had detailed an attempted escape by twelve prisoners. Peel quoted from the report:

> '"… and had not their concerted plan been discovered before they had succeeded, very serious consequences would have been the result, as many of them had determined on desperate measures."'

William Strang was implicated, leaving Peel 'under the necessity of rescinding my intention of transferring the Prisoner to the General Penitentiary …' and, instead, Strang and the other convicts were sent to the hulks.

Strang's father petitioned Robert Peel on 3 August 1829, writing from 88, Jamaica Street, Glasgow. He asked for his son to be allowed to stay in England

and to be separated from hardened criminals because, being only twenty years old, he would still be a young man at the end of this sentence. Appended is a letter from W. Rose, Governor of the National Gaol of Scotland, Edinburgh, dated the following day; it concerns the attempted break-out of which Strang had been part. Once the plan had been discovered and Strang was separated from the other prisoners Strang 'very readily and candidly disclosed the whole proceedings' Rose wrote but added, 'He appears a very thoughtless youth, easily biased, and too much swayed by his companions in crime.'

Strang was sent to the *Justitia* hulk at Woolwich but his behaviour was far from perfect. Whilst there, papers taken from him which explain how to make counterfeit coins. (See Chapter 7).

An undated note from John H. Capper, Superintendent of Prisons and the Hulks, stated that Strang's conduct had been:

> '… so very bad since his arrival on board the Hulks that his earliest transportation is desirable – detected with Plans for Coining – Clothing & Money concealed on Shore for the purpose when at Labour of making his escape.'

The Home Office case note reads, 'Transport him RP [Robert Peel], October 24.'

Strang sailed to New South Wales on the *Mermaid* transport ship in December 1829. He received his certificate of freedom on 20 May 1836.

Essex born **Elizabeth Wheatley** (or Weatley) was twenty years old when she stood trial at Surrey Summer Assizes held at Guildford in August 1832, accused of receiving stolen goods. Found guilty, she was sentenced to fourteen years transportation. A petition sent from five supporters, including the prosecutrix, Elizabeth Faulkner, did not question the justice of the sentence but was 'deeply lamenting its fatal severity'. The supporters wrote that this case:

> '… is an unfortunate Exemplification of an instance where a young woman of humble but honest parentage in the Country, comes up to Town inexperienced & a child comparatively in years – procures respectable situations, has her affections gained by a bad character – who practices upon her simplicity – becomes his dupe & expiates her life upon the Gallows – <u>for the crime of Another.</u>'

The person to whom the petitioners allude was almost certainly George Wheatley. He had been found guilty of stealing the watch which she had been found guilty of receiving.

Elizabeth's Home Office petition file contains two letters from 'G.W.'. Both appear to have penned whilst he, George Wheatley, and Elizabeth were confined awaiting trial. It is possible that the letters were passed to the Home Office by Elizabeth's supporters to show George's influence (and guilt) or discovered on Elizabeth, George or one of their visitors. The first letter is dated 3 August 1832:

'I am sorry to find that you are so ill I hope that you will get better before our trial comes on. I have seeing my mother and I asked her to get a counceler but she says that it will be on no use as she as being to Mrs Folkeners the prosecutor is not a going [illegible]... she only wants her watch back and if she can have it she will make a [illegible] in the indictment and that will get us of all together. My mother as being to her and she will do all she can for to get us both of as she does not mean to hurt us she as told my mother so – I named to my mother about some things for you but she will not do anything for you untill she knows whether we are married or not and if she thought that we as so she would consider you as one of the familay and would do anything for you as laid in her power I asked her to come to see you she said she might but she did not say positively that she would she bought me some tobaccoo and a trifle of money as it was not much I have not sent you any but I expect my sister to see me and if she does she will bring me some money and if she does I will send you some as soon as I get it I expect that my brother will be down at Guildford a purpose to hear what you mean to say at your trial to see if you mean to tell all about it if you do it will cost us both at once my friends are all afraid that you will as they have being told that you mean to tell the truth about it we shall not whant for anything while we are at Guildford as my brother will be there I hope that you will not say anything for your sake as mine as well. Your sister as being to me this [illegible] time I expect Mary in tomorrow to see me Matilda is a going to try to get me some sugar and coffee in if she can she told me that she as got a note that I sent you she is a going to Mrs Folkener and a going to tell her about a Fred gieving me the watch your Sister is a going to send you some things to go down in. She told me that Mary as got some of the tickets as Mrs Holloway give her after I have seen your Sister tomorrow and she lets me know about Mrs Folkener and then we shall know later what we shall have to do and I will let you know I hope that you will make your selfe comfortable as well as you can in your situation and that you will be all right for things before you go down to Guildford so no more at present from your Affectionate lover G.W.'

It's highly likely Elizabeth's illness was related to early stages of pregnancy: she gave birth to twins six months later. The second letter is undated, and Wheatley is:

'… very sorry that you think that I whant to lay it all to you… If you think you think that it will be better for you to throw it upon me do so I would rather go out of the country myselfe than you should God knows I have done every thing that I can do for you and have spoke well of you to my friends what more can I do for you at present, I should a thought that you wonts a being the last person to have throwd in my face that what you have done for me but there I do not care that it is come to this my back is broad enough to bare it and if you wish to send me out of the Country do it in Gods name I did not think that you had such a opinion of me you sister as being to see me this day and she brought me a clean shirt and some Coffee and Sugar they have being to the prosecutor and she says that she will plead for mercy for us and will say what she did before and as to Fred what she will say will not hurt us and let me still persuade you not to say any more than what you are oblige to say I tell you as a Husband and a friend to you although you do think I am no friend to you true and patients will for come it you will find that the less that you say the better it will be for us do as you please I do not care which way it is if you like to send me away do – you mention about your sleeping in the front cell I do not I sleep in one of the back cells so I cannot look out to you I wish I could, Your sister is a coming to see you on Monday I hope that you will make your selfe comfortable as I will do everything that I can to make you so. You said I ought to sent you a trifle of money I have had none only one shilling that my mother gave to me and that I used for some bread to the wardsman a loaf a day is not much if I had any I would send it to you with pleasure I think you are a Silly Girl to give the letter to your Sister I wish you to send me word what you mean to say at your trial let me know if you will [illegible] From your affectionate lover G.W.'

Despite the efforts of Elizabeth Wheatley's supporters, the annotation on the Home Office case states, 'Abroad', and she was transported on the female transport ship, *Diana*, leaving England in December 1832 and arriving in New South Wales, May 1833.

During the voyage, on 4 February 1833, Elizabeth Wheatley gave birth to twins, a boy and a girl. However the ship's surgeon and superintendent's sick list shows the boy, George, died four days later 'unable to swallow or suckle since birth'. Under the name of Elizabeth Whately, she had been on the sick list since 2 January, seemingly with issues related to her pregnancy and she was not discharged until 25 February. At least three other entries from early March to early April show Elizabeth on the sick list again suffering from costiveness, in other words, constipation.

It seems Elizabeth's daughter was named Georgiana, presumably after her father, although George's name does not appear to be on the records. She was christened at St John's, Parramatta on 7 July 1833. Her surname is spelt 'Wheatly'.[4]

Elizabeth married Peter Ashe in 18 May 1837 at St Thomas, Port Macquarie, New South Wales. Her age is given as twenty-four, (born 1813), and his as twenty-seven[5] and during this time she appears to have been using variations on her original name, calling herself Ann Wheatley or Ann Price. It's possible this is the same Peter Ashe, convict, who arrived in New South Wales on the *Fairlie* in February 1834. He had been tried at Leicester Quarter Sessions, August 1833, and received a fourteen year sentence though his crime is unknown. He applied for permission to marry 'Elizabeth Wheathy' and his ticket of leave was gained in 1841, the latter reported in The New South Wales Government Gazette of 23 April 1841.

New South Wales records that show Elizabeth Wheatley obtained her certificate of freedom in September 1846 and gives her alias, Ann Price.

George Wheatley was transported on the *Waterloo* in March 1833, arriving in New South Wales in August of that year. According to New South Wales archives, he obtained his ticket of leave passport in 1845 and his Conditional Pardon in June 1848.

George Whitchurch and **Elizabeth Jones** were in service at Lamer Park, near St Albans, Hertfordshire. Whitchurch was butler and Jones both cook and house-keeper at the country home of Levi Ames, who also kept a London house in Hereford Street, Park Lane. When Whitchurch and Jones were apprehended for 'sending out' a piece of pork and other provisions, Ames pressed for their prosecution. Found guilty at Hertfordshire's Quarter

Sessions on Monday, 14 January 1828, they were both sentenced to fourteen years transportation.

The severity of their sentence shocked not only the offenders but others in the courtroom and many members of the public, who felt it was disproportionate to the crime. On the following Saturday, 19 January, the *Herts Mercury and General Advertiser* newspaper carried a letter to the Editor, referring to the report of the County Sessions. It was signed, 'A LOOKER ON'. The writer claimed to be one of the vast majority of ordinary people, all perplexed and unable to understand the reasons behind such a sentence. The outcome was particularly puzzling he (or she) wrote, because the Trial Chairman, Lord Dacre, had a reputation for compassion and Christian values. The letter suggested the public had complained that the jury's views had not been taken in to account when the sentence was reached. Further, Peel's recent 'Act' was primarily levelled at clerks and those who held responsible positions, designed to deter them from embezzling; it would not have the desired effect on servants who took a piece of fruit.

The writer added it was the job of the jury to pronounce on guilt or otherwise and, although they recommended mercy for Whitchurch and Jones, that recommendation had been treated with disdain and not mentioned when the Chairman passed what was the heaviest of sentences. The letter ended with the writer expressing pleasure that appeals for mercy were likely to be made, suggested by the prisoners' counsel, agreed by the jury, and supported by everyone wanting to see a fair outcome.

The same day, the *Herts Mercury and General Advertiser* ran an article under the section 'Herts Epiphany Sessions', using the heading 'Caution to Servants'. Here the paper stated it was their belief that the Whitchurch and Jones case was the first in the county in which this part of the Statute has been used and therefore, the paper felt the case merited the coverage they had given it, serving as a warning to the public. The report noted the prosecution, led by Mr Broderick, told the jury that it was not the value of the items but the principle of justice that was at stake.

At the trial, evidence for the prosecution was given by Whitchurch and Jones's fellow servants and included the chief and under gamekeeper, under-butler, the coachman and the kitchen maid, along with two butchers who were father and son. The newspaper account told how the other servants had observed parcels being sent out by Whitchurch and Jones on previous occasions and heard noises coming from Whitchurch's room late at night. When Whitchurch was apprehended, the gamekeeper and under-butler took the packages from him. He had resisted at first but when the packages were opened in front of Mrs Ames, Whitchurch claimed he had bought the meat and that the other items were legitimately obtained.

The following day, Whitchurch approached the butcher and asked him to confirm his story but the butcher refused and although the butler then tried to leave Lamer Park, he was caught and returned. After offering various explanations, including one that Jones had lent him the meat which he intended to replace for his mistress, finally Whitchurch confessed.

Jones and Whitchurch's counsel, Mr Ryland, suggested that the other servants held a grudge against Whitchurch because of a previous incident concerning beer. The prisoners said nothing in their defence, but Whitchurch's good character was confirmed by Thomas Hall Plomer, son of the late Master of the Rolls, and for whose mother, Lady Plomer, Whitchurch had worked. The report concludes by telling how both Whitchurch and Jones were distraught on hearing the sentence and a female friend of Elizabeth Jones fainted and needed to be carried out of the courtroom.

From the petitions available, it appears the appeals for mercy for Whitchurch and Jones were lead separately, by two men: George Cathrow for Whitchurch and Henry Robinson Junior, for Jones. Robinson, a banker with Wright & Company, employed Elizabeth Jones's sister as cook and housekeeper. Cathrow[6] was a jury member at the trial of Whitchurch and Jones and co-owned Hoddesdon brewery with John Christie.

On 22 January 1828, Cathrow wrote from Hoddesdon Brewery to S.M. Phillipps at the Home Office, outlining Whitchurch and Jones's trial and saying they were convicted of sending out 'provisions of a very trifling description to private friends … for which they were capitally indicted under Mr Peel's late Act…' He described how he had become involved in the case, never having seen the prisoners before but being on the Grand Jury, had:

> '… heard the whole charge and could not consent to send them to trial being of opinion the transaction was not done with <u>Felonious intent</u> in which one other juryman concurred[.] of course we were out voted…'

The Jury strongly recommended mercy.

Cathrow had no doubt the case was being used as 'a warning to other servants who have had such latitude given them by the nobility etc etc that they had scarcely thought it an offence now...' He offered to take in Whitchurch as a servant and described how he had taken in people before.

> '...about 7 years ago I was induced to take a footman in to my family who was discharged by his former Master Mr Jacobs of Hadham (without a character) for the same offence but was not prosecuted[.] he proved a faithful steady man lived with me several years and died in my service.'

The footman was not the first to be shown Cathrow's benevolence, and Cathrow told how seven years prior to that incident he employed in the brewery, a 'young man induced by a bad girl to rob his Master's till'. The young man was imprisoned and publicly whipped and, Cathrow informed Phillipps, 'I am happy to assure you he has turned out a most deserving worthy member of society and is still in this concern'. The young man's brother was employed in the brewery and had turned to Cathrow for help. Of Whitchurch and Jones Cathrow wrote, 'The whole County seem interested in their fate'. The back of his letter carries a Home Office annotation, 'Penitentiary'.

At the beginning of February 1828, Henry Robinson Junior wrote to Home Secretary, Robert Peel, regarding the case of Elizabeth Jones. He stated that he had never met Elizabeth but he knew of the case through her sister, who had asked him to plead, 'and the case seemed to me so peculiarly hard that I should not refuse to submit it to your favourable consideration...' He pointed out that, whilst Whitchurch had sent a box from the house, which held pork minced meat, apples and a hare, Jones had played a minor role, in that 'the only part of the offence in which she appears to have been implicated was that of having given the Butler the hare...' Despite the jury recommending mercy, magistrates had handed both offenders the same severe sentence. Pressing Jones's reasons for clemency, Robinson added:

> '... it may be considered some extenuation of the offence, that she had been ordered to throw away two hares which had become unfit for the Table'.

Robinson detailed Jones's considerable service working 'in families of the first respectability'. For five and a half years, Jones had been employed by the late Honourable Andrew Foley of Worcestershire; she had spent three with Herbert Turner DCL in Chesterfield Street, London; one year with Lady

Jones of South Audley Street, also in London; one year with the Honourable Captain Poulett RN who 'commands the flag ship in the Medway'; one year with Moffat Mills; a further year with the Honourable Captain Poulett; and almost two years for Mr Levi Ames, the prosecutor.

Robinson told the Home Secretary that he was collecting certificates of good conduct from Jones's previous employers, but 'Mr Mills is unfortunately abroad'. He stated Ames refused to sign any petition calling for mercy and noted Ames held a resentment which 'betrays itself' in his reply to Robinson:

> '... for he throws doubts on her previous honesty and charges her with being habitually drunk and having consequently last winter evidently set fire to her bed and obliged the whole family to turn out at two in the morning in one of the severest frosts possible.
>
> '... it will I am sure immediately occur to you Sir to ask why after such flagrant misconduct she was allowed to remain another year in his service, and up to the moment of this paltry theft. She could scarcely have been so bad as he represented.
>
> '... a punishment so enormously disproportionate to the value of the object stolen is less likely to operate as a warning to servants than it is to deter Masters from prosecuting. As a banker I have too many reasons to know that embezzlement and forgery have frequently escaped with impunity from the dread of inflicting on the culprits the certain and awful fate that a prosecution would have inevitably entailed.'

Robinson had almost certainly sent his petition via Colonel Graham Foster Piggott MP, because on 13 February 1828, Piggott wrote to Robert Peel thanking him for considering the petitions of Elizabeth Jones and Whitchurch which he presented for Messrs Wright & Company, Bankers. Around the same time Lord Dacre replied to a Home Office enquiry. In it, he confirmed that he agreed with the facts in the petitions of Whitchurch and Jones, inasmuch as they were consistent with what he had heard at the trial. He also agreed with the comment attributed to him, regarding the effect on the previous good character of Whitchurch. He continued:

> 'The consideration which appeared to make a strong impression upon the magistrates present (who were numerous, and concurring in the sentence with only two or, at most three dissentients) was the

importance of the example – and this impression and strengthened by the circumstance of Whitchurch having attempted to induce the butcher, who served the family of the Prosecutor, to declare that he had sold to the prisoner the article which constituted the principal subject matter of the indictment – this fact came out in evidence … I do not, however, hesitate to say that I have considered the sentence a severe one; tho' I show'd at little hesitate to contend that it was a just one and likely to be attended with beneficial effects. In fact I conceive that such effects have been already in a considerable degree, produced, and under that impression I must beg to leave it to your own consideration, to decide, in how far a mitigation of the sentence is to be recommended under the circumstances of the case.'

Elizabeth Jones's sentence was commuted from transportation for fourteen years to imprisonment at the Penitentiary, where she arrived on 19 February, while Whitchurch remained in Hertfordshire County Gaol. A separate Home Office annotation notes, 'Any further mitigation must depend on good conduct'.

According to a petition sent by members of both the Grand Jury and Petty Jury, on both servants' behalf, the only articles found in the prisoners' possession, taken from their master, was a 'hand of pork and a hare the value of which could not exceed a few shillings'. It pointed out fellow-servant, John Miles, who was:

'a material witness for the prosecution admitted upon cross examination that he had once quarrelled with the prisoner Whitchurch for not allowing him and the other servants so much strong beer (of which as Butler he had the charge) as they wished for; and in his general manner of giving evidence evinced a feeling of animosity against the said prisoner.'

The petition stated Thomas Hall Plomer, confirmed Whitchurch had been employed by Lady Plomer for almost three years and was a 'faithful industrious and honest servant in whom the greatest confidence had been placed and which confidence had never been abused…' It was noted Plomer had 'voluntarily travelled a considerable distance' in order to give the reference, and that Whitchurch had gone to work at the Plomers' house with an excellent character from his previous employer.

The jury understood George Whitchurch to have been one of five children born to a respectable grocer, deceased, who traded in Huntingdon for 'upwards of 40 years'. One of his sisters, Fanny, was a lady's maid and housekeeper for 'upwards of 15 years' in the employment of Mr Newman in Lyme, Dorset and 'much esteemed' by her employer. Another sister, Martha, had recently left a similar situation owing to ill health and two brothers were respectably employed as coachmen. Whitchurch had lived in service as butler to Matthias Woodmason of Belcamp near Dublin, for 'upwards of nine years' before going into business for five years, though no details of that business are given. He then joined Lady Plomer at Canons Park, Edgware.

Whitchurch was a widower with two children aged fourteen and ten:

> '... a kind affectionate and careful parent and good Christian and
> that the articles so taken by him were actually sent to Mrs Collins,
> and another Female person of respectability in London, as a pres-
> ent, in return for some act of kindness shewn by them to his said
> children.'

According to the petition, the parents of Elizabeth Jones were 'upwards of 80 years of age'. They had lived all their lives with the Foley family in Newport, Hertfordshire where Elizabeth too had lived until she left to work for Herbert Jenner in Chislehurst, Kent. She remained in service there for three years, then worked for Lord Shaftesbury the same amount of time before being employed by Captain Pawlett (or Poulett). The petitioners explained Elizabeth changed jobs 'not through any misconduct, but a desire to better herself ...' rising from kitchen maid to housekeeper. It was claimed both Whitchurch and Jones had integrity: they didn't steal to sell on the goods. However, the severe sentence, to make them a public example, had put them 'upon a level with the most hardened and notorious offenders'. As a consequence, their families and friends were also suffering.

The petitioners concluded by expressing their satisfaction that the sentence 'has already had the effect intended by the Court of Quarter Sessions of holding forth to others the Enormity of similar offences'. It was signed by fourteen men of the Grand Jury and twelve men of the Petty Jury. The first juror's signature is that of George Cathrow. It also bore the signatures of Marianne Plomer, Thomas Hall Plomer and Archer Ryland 'counsel for the Prisoners'.

On 14 May 1828, George Cathrow again wrote to S.M. Phillipps at the Home Office, informing him he had heard an order had been sent to the county gaol that day for Whitchurch's immediate transportation. Cathrow explained he had 'interested myself' only because of the prisoner's previous good character and because Cathrow was reserving a job for Whitchurch 'at a salary of 40 guineas per ann.' which, he reminded Phillipps, he had told him before. He continued, 'I hope and trust there is some mistake respecting him ...' and confirmed that his opinion of Whitchurch remained unchanged, having made many thorough enquiries. The only exception was 'what has been reported from his <u>late vindictive master</u>'. He reminded Phillipps of the letter he had received from him, dated 12 February 1828, in which Phillipps told him:

> '... that Mr Peel upon full consideration of all the circumstances of the case has felt himself warranted in detaining Whitchurch in the County Gaol at Hertford and that he is not to <u>undergo transportation</u> on which authority I have relied implicitly...'

Two days later, W. Willson wrote from the County Gaol in Hertford to John H. Capper, Superintendent of the prison hulks, confirming that Whitchurch had not been removed to the hulks but 'the others will be removed on Monday next ...'

In January of the following year, George Cathrow sent another letter to Phillipps at the Home Office, drawing his attention to the case of Whitchurch. He reminded him that Whitchurch had been in prison for more than a year and that Cathrow had already offered to employ him if Whitchurch was liberated. He suggested the time Whitchurch had served was enough to see that justice had been done, but although the Home Office answered on 21 January, Whitchurch remained in gaol.

An undated Home Department memo to Robert Peel, probably sent by S.M. Phillipps, notes that the two prisoners in this case were tried by Lord Dacre in his capacity as Chairman and points out that Cathrow's letter petitions for Whitchurch alone. It continues:

> 'The only question is whether for such an offence, and the sentence being 14 years transportation, one years imprisonment is sufficient.'

Robert Peel replies 'I think he right to remain <u>two years</u> in prison. RP'.

In early October of the same year, Henry Robinson Junior was again in correspondence with Phillipps, writing from his address in Henrietta Street,

London. This time he forwarded a petition from Jones. He drew attention to the fact that he had been told 'about 20 months ago' of the commutation of Jones's sentence from transportation to imprisonment at the Penitentiary. He reiterated that Jones had 'given away' things of small value and that her master, Levy Ames, was 'a person of Fortune.' He outlined Jones's previous work history and had asked all her former employers for character references. All confirmed her excellent character except Lord Shaftesbury who declined to write on the grounds that he had employed her a long time ago but had given Jones a good reference at the time.

Robinson explained that he employed Jones's sister as cook who herself was 'an honest and excellent servant'. He claimed that he believed all that was written in Jones's petition and was sure she was suffering both mentally and physically from her near two years imprisonment. The Home Secretary's annotation reads, 'Let her remain in the Penitentiary for the present'.

On 21 January 1830, George Whitchurch sent a letter from his cell to the Visiting Magistrates of Hertfordshire County Gaol, reminding them he had been in gaol 'for upwards of two years' and that he had been on the list to be transported in May 1828. Transportation had not taken place because Mr Willson, the Governor of the Gaol, had been told by John H. Capper to keep Whitchurch there until further instructions from the Home Secretary. He appealed to the magistrates to recommend him for mitigation of his sentence 'for the sake of his two unfortunate children who are now supported by a sister of your Petitioner'. He was sure, he told the magistrates, that the prison governor would speak in his favour 'as since Petitioner's confinement he has frequently had juvenile offenders placed under his care by order of the Governor and has frequently taught them to read …'

Two days later, the Visiting Magistrates at the County gaol forwarded Whitchurch's petition to the Home Office. They took the opportunity to state that they believed the facts which Whitchurch had written:

'… we can also assure you that the Gaoler's Reports to us of the prisoners conduct and behaviour during his confinement have been highly favourable to him. We beg leave to recommend his case for your consideration.'

The letter is signed by Thomas Daniell, George Brassley and John Green. The pencilled Home Office notes on the back of these letters first asks, 'Why was this man not transported?' and, 'To be pardoned Feb 10.' The Home Office reply to the magistrates was sent 11 February 1830.

On 7 February 1830, George Cathrow had raised Whitchurch's case again with the Home Office, writing that Whitchurch's 'conduct I am informed by Mr Wilson as well as the Rev Mr Lloyd, has been most exemplary'.

A Home Office pencil note on the back of Cathrow's letter states, 'I think inquiry should again be made at the Penitentiary respecting the <u>female prisoner</u>'. That enquiry was made and on 9 February 1830, Chapman, the governor of the General Penitentiary at Millbank, replied in a response to a request for a report on Elizabeth Jones. Chapman stated his 'sincere pleasure in bearing testimony to her unvaried exemplary conduct ever since her admission into this Institution, never having in the slightest degree given cause of reprehension.' He noted, 'The Poor woman suffers exceedingly from severe rheumatic affection' which he considered was probably the result of being used to hot temperatures as a cook 'and the difference of temperature she has been unavoidably subject to here'. On the back of this letter, the Home Office annotation reads, 'To be pardoned Feb 10'.

On 12 February 1830, Cathrow wrote again to the Home Office saying he had 'communicated the contents to Whitchurch today who was truly grateful for the leniency shown him and I hope he will evince the same by his future good conduct.' To emphasise his faith in this final statement, Cathrow reiterated how Whitchurch had taught other prisoners to read, a task at which 'he has been very successful.'

According to a Home Office note, free pardons for both Whitchurch and Jones were prepared for the King's signature on 11 February 1830.

Mention of Whitchurch and Jones's case appears in a book published in 1829, *Friendly Advice to My Poor Neighbours: In a Series of Cottage Tales and Dialogues* by 'A Member of the Church of England.' In a section entitled 'Miscellaneous Facts; extracted from the public newspapers' and under the sub-heading 'Caution to Servants' and attributed to 'London Paper' the case is outlined and the article continues:

'The indictment was framed under a recent act of Parliament, for inflicting more severe punishments upon servants convicted of robbing their employers. The counsel for the Prosecution said, that it was not the value of the articles stolen but a sense of public justice, and the necessity of checking a great and increasing evil, which induced the prosecutor to bring the prisoners to the bar.'

Chapter 5

Words from the General Penitentiary, Millbank, London

Writing *The Criminal Prisons of London and Scenes of Prison Life* in the middle of the nineteenth century, Mayhew and Binny categorised the many and overcrowded prisons in London as: State or Political prisons eg. Tower of London; Civil or Debtors prisons eg. Queens Bench; and Criminal Prisons. Petitions sent from the latter category of prisons are those used in this book.

Mayhew and Binny further divide the 'Criminal Prison' category in to pre- and post-conviction: Post-conviction consists of 'Convict Prisons' and 'Correctional Prisons', the former defined as being used prior to transportation or for 'penal service' and includes the General Penitentiary and the prison hulks; the latter includes Houses of Correction and Bridewells, which generally housed thieves and vagrants with shorter sentences.

'Detentional Prisons' are defined as those detaining people before conviction. The 'post-committal' category includes Newgate Prison.

Until 1823, all those convicted of committing a crime were put in a common jail together, from 'the simple novice to the artful adept...' regardless of their previous record. In an attempt to minimise the risk of the more experienced criminal corrupting the less hardened offender, legislation was put in to place to impose separation by level of offence. In their petitions for mercy, prisoners or their supporters often cite the desire to keep themselves away from the corrupting influence of hardened offenders as a reason for a reduction in sentence or wanting to be sent to a particular institution.

After several years of planning and construction, the General Penitentiary at Millbank, London, was fully opened in 1821. Built on the banks of the Thames, its scale and design was intended to deter future offenders. In *An Account of the General Penitentiary at Millbank* published in 1828, George Holford describes it as having:

> 'an outer lodge and boundary wall, surrounding about fifteen acres of ground, and of six Pentagons with a chapel in the middle,

covering and enclosing about seven acres of ground, and having eighteen towers at their external angles or corners.'

Over thirty years later Henry Mayhew and John Binny write:

'This immense yellow-brown mass of brick-work is surrounded by a low wall of the same material, above which is seen a multitude of small squarish windows and a series of diminutive roofs of slate, like low retreating foreheads ... an ungainly combination of the mad-house with the fortress style of building for it has a series of martello like towers, one at each end of its many angles, and was originally surrounded by a moat, whilst its long lines of embrasure-like windows are barred after the fashion of Bedlam and St Luke's.

'At night the prison is nothing but a dark, shapeless structure, the hugeness of which is made more apparent by the bright yellow specks which shine from the casements'.

But the radial design of the Penitentiary proved unsatisfactory. Chosen in order that each wing, and all cells, could be seen by the warders in the central hexagon, the building's vast size and multiple-storey structure became its weakness. Further, it had been built on marsh land, bought from the Marquis of Salisbury in 1799 at a cost of £12,000, and damp became a problem within a short time. Not only was this to be detrimental to the fabric of the building, but to the health of the prisoners, which was soon compromised due also to the poor ventilation of the building.

Emphasis was placed on religious instruction, which it was hoped would lead to prisoner reform, but Mayhew and Binny considered there had been 'undue reliance' on such by one prison Governor, 'a reverend Gentleman'; it was easy for prisoners to say things whilst imprisoned that, when freed, would be forgotten. In order to minimise the potential corruption of, and collusion between, prisoners, prison routines were altered as the Penitentiary moved into its second full decade.

The experience of three prisoners, in letters written to family in the 1830s, give further insight and great detail about life in the Penitentiary. The letters were included in the Home Office correspondence relating to their petitions.

William Richard Glazier (or **Glasier**), a 52-year-old conveyancer, had been found guilty of uttering a forged Power of Attorney at the Old Bailey October Sessions of 1832, and was sentenced to transportation for life. (The prosecutor was the Bank of England.) Glazier's reasons for clemency included the fact that he believed he'd acted honestly but had pleaded guilty on his friends' advice, his previous character having been good. He was ordered to the Penitentiary and entered there on 11 December 1832. He would receive a conditional pardon in October the following year, the condition being that Glazier should leave the country before 10 November and not return.

On 27 June 1833 Glazier sent a letter to his wife, 'My dear Betsy'. After acknowledging the news sent in her previous letter he tells her he has been:

'… very unwell in the Infirmary here, for <u>twelve weeks</u> and altho' I have the most able Medical skill attention and kindness from the Medical Gentlemen and continue to receive every kindness from the Governor Chaplain and every officer, I do not feel any better and fear I shall not when my age is considered and while I remain here.'

He asks his brother to meet with other friends and supporters to petition the Home Secretary, Lord Melbourne, so Glazier can go abroad to restore his health:

'enabling me to support you & our dear children … I am most anxious to go out to Van Diemen's Land to my good friend Mr Nicholson who wished me to accompany him (before he left England) Oh if the Almighty would direct his Lordship to grant me this favour I am sure my poor mind would become tranquil, and my Body discontinue to waste away'.

He tells her he is too 'agitated' to write as he would like, and as he normally does.

Almost certainly mindful that his letters are being read, when remarking that if his brother and friend Kimpton want to see the prisoner to talk about securing mitigation, he states, 'I am quite certain that neither our worthy Governor or Chaplain would refuse their request.'

Glazier's letter is written on Penitentiary paper which bears printed instructions in the margins for the benefit of the recipient regarding the letters they might write to the inmates in return. It reminds the reader the prisoner has been allowed to write and receive letters in order that they can:

'… keep up a connexion with the respectable part of their family or friends (to whom it is hoped they may be reconciled or reunited when they shall be restored to Society at the end of their imprisonment) and not that they may hear the news of the day or be amused with the accounts of Public matters, with which they can have no concern.'

Therefore, those corresponding are discouraged from mentioning 'subjects of this nature.' It informs the recipient the governor or chaplain read all letters received by the prison and with this in mind, the letters should not be 'of unnecessary length' nor 'very frequent' because the prisoner bears the cost through deductions from their earnings.

James David White, originally from Taunton in Devon, was 21 years old when he was tried at the Old Bailey, April Sessions, 1836. The previous year, White, a solicitor's clerk, had forged a cheque for £212 in the name of one of his employers, William Osbaldeston. Found guilty, White was sentenced to transportation for life, and ordered first to the *Leviathan* hulk at Portsmouth. On 7 May 1836, following petitioning from many respectable supporters, his sentence was reduced to fourteen years and he was ordered to the General Penitentiary. On paper bearing the same instructions in the margin as that used by Glazier, White wrote to his mother, brother and sisters on 2 December 1836. In his letter, he gives comprehensive details of the prison routine and a clear insight in to his mental state.

'Six long & dreary months have passed since I have seen you & I am now if possible more miserable than ever – this arises partly from my imprisonment but chiefly from the opportunity I have had of looking in to myself & comparing my past conduct with what it should have been – and also what I am now to what I might have been had I listened to the good advice you one & all of you were at all times ready to give me.'

After assuring his family he has seen 'the error of my ways' he tells them that he will rectify his behaviour in the future:

'The Bible which I have made my constant study during my confinement however holds out a cheering balm to the greatest sinner.'

Perhaps emphasising his serious intent, he quotes several lines from the Bible. White asks his family apply again for mercy through his supporters:

'… if nothing can be done I would beg of you to get me sent out of the Country for should I remain here (3½ years) the usual time for persons with my sentence I shall be cast upon the world without any hope of employment… & thus every hope of re-establishing myself in that Society to which I before belonged will be at an end.'

Describing how he spends his time, White first tells how the Prison is divided in Pentagons, and the Pentagons into wards, each ward containing 32 prisoners:

'At present we rise at ¼ past seven o'clock & after washing the morning Hymn sing & a portion of scripture selected by the Chaplain is read by one of the Prisoners with suitable prayers – after which we proceed to work.'

He tells his family he is employed tailoring, 'at which I can work pretty well'. Three times a day, in half-hour sessions, the prisoners work 'at a Machine for supplying the Prison with water', and after each session are allowed to walk in the yard for a quarter of an hour.

Breakfast is at eight o'clock:

'½ a lb of Bread with a Pint of Milk & water with an ounce of flour to thicken it – at one – 4 times a week we get 6 ounces of Beef with Potatoes & half a lb of Bread and a Pint of liquor in which the Beef is boiled - twice a week we get a quart of Soup with Potatoes & Bread & on Saturdays a Pound of Bread and Cheese - we are locked up for the night at present immediately at 4 o'clock & for supper get another Pint of Milk and Water and Bread as in the morning – but before locking up prayers are read and the Evening Hymn sung – thus you will see what with not being allowed to speak to each other & the night fifteen hours long not a third of which can I sleep the time passes wretchedly enough.'

White explains the prison routine times are different in summer, with the prisoners rising at half past five and locking-up taking place at seven in the evening. The prisoners attend 'school in the Passages of the Prison' on two evenings a week after supper. Here they face questions about the Bible and church catechism with prisoners who are able to read, write and 'cypher' teaching those prisoners from the same ward who cannot.

The prisoners attend chapel once on Sundays. On Wednesdays, they attend twice; in the morning 'when the Chaplain lectures on the gospel for the ensuing Sunday' and in the afternoon they are:

'questioned on the Bible – the Chaplain is a truly pious Man & is
at all times ready to give information to those who may not understand what they read in the Bible.'

There are plenty of opportunities for communication between the prisoners
and the chaplain and governor. However, a prison officer is:

'at all times with each Ward to prevent talking and so strict are the
rules it may keep a prisoner some time longer than the usual period
should he be reported for so doing.'

Turning back to his prison sentence, White beseeches his family 'by every
means in your power' to help secure his freedom:

'I shall not be able to see you or write again for 6 months but am
permitted to receive a Letter from you every Month which I hope
someone or other of you will not neglect.'

He assures them his health is, and has been good, throughout his imprisonment, and ends the letter by sending his 'sincere thanks to Mr Suter' who
has enquired after him and asks his family to 'remember me to Mr Hickman,
Mr Eliot and all friends at Hackney.' He adds at the bottom:

'I am permitted to write this while my fellow Prisoners are taking
exercise in the Yard & must therefore excuse all imperfections.'

When the parents of 14-year-old **Thomas Graham** received a letter from
their son, dated 21 December 1837, the Penitentiary paper it was written on
bore the same instructions as those the White and Glazier families would
have read. Thomas, a servant, had been tried at the Central Criminal Court,
Old Bailey, six months earlier and found guilty of stealing in a dwelling
house. Sentenced to a year in the Penitentiary followed by transportation
for life, he entered the Penitentiary on 23 June, and the letter his parents
received is probably written with the help of a fellow prisoner or the chaplain, given the mature sentiments it expresses.

Opening, 'Dear Father & Mother' Thomas Graham expresses great pen-
itence and writes:

'There is Nothing I can Charge you with as Not having done your
duty towards me I Charge everything upon myself and not on you

for surely had I studied and practised my own duty better I had never planted thorns on your pillows … Some religious impression was raised in my mind on reading A Little Book entitled the Sinners Friend which was put into my hand by the Worthy Chaplain of this institution & I desire that impression may be Lasting & effectual so that at lenght I may become A Comfort to my Friends and a worthy member of Christs Church…

'I am provided with all things necessary for life and Godliness and that my Circumstances are more favourable more Comfortable that Can reasonably be expected; let this be a Comfort to you as I know it must and Will …'

However, he continues that he has been told 'by the Authorities of this Institution' that 'shortly' he is to be transported:

'The idea of bidding Adieu to my Kind and aged Parents of quitting all [illegible] familiar scenes of my youth and the objects of my affection is verry distressing to my mind …'

He asks for the forgiveness of his master and signs the letter 'I remain your now Affectionate thoug once undutiful son Thomas Graham.'

Thomas Graham's parents, William and Sarah, lived at Westway's Yard, Providence Street, St Helier, Jersey and they didn't receive his letter until 11 January 1838. Two days later, however, they forwarded their son's letter to Edward Allison, his master and prosecutor, to ask if he and his wife would help 'keep our unfortunate Boy, from exile'. The Grahams mention their son's recent letter had taken time to reach them 'by some mistake' but add they have replied to him 'by this post'.

Edward Wenman Allison supported Thomas Graham's case, stating he felt partly to blame because he had left too much temptation in front of the boy, and he was willing to employ him again, if freed. With the Penitentiary Governor, D. Nihill, confirming the prisoner had been 'well behaved', Thomas Graham received a free pardon on 2 June 1838.

Chapter 6

Forgery

Forgery can be considered to fall in to three categories: Forgery of documents (e.g. Powers of Attorney, Wills); Forgery of money (e.g. Bank notes or making counterfeit coins); Uttering (i.e. possessing or presenting forged notes or coins).

All three categories were capital offences until August 1832, after which only the forging of Wills and Powers of Attorney for the transference of stock and receipt of dividends remained a capital offence until later that decade. Whilst the stability and security of the country were deemed to depend on the Crown, counterfeiting coin was considered High Treason, but by the 1830s this view had changed.

It was vital to the country's interest to protect its currency and support its means of trading but bank notes were easy to forge and the number of small independent banks printing their own notes added to the problem of control. As a consequence, convictions for forgery were rarely commuted, though the death sentence was replaced with transportation for life when it ceased to be a capital offence.

In the early decades of the nineteenth century, gangs of coiners were prevalent – the Vauxhall coiners, Greenwich coiners – but passing counterfeit coins was usually considered to be a woman's offence as it was easier to pass off small coins when shopping; similarly, receiving was easier for women. For first time offenders, a maximum of six months imprisonment was applied, increasing to two years for a second offence. However, if caught a third time, the offender could be capitally convicted as this was deemed to be treasonable.

John Hill Wagstaff was taken into custody on 25 March 1824, accused of forging an order for the payment of £250 purporting to be the order of William Ridley & Co, with intent to defraud Benjamin Bond and others. A handbill printed by C. Eastman of Cheapside had offered a 100 Guineas reward for anyone apprehending Hill who, the bill announced, had committed 'divers forgeries on several of the London Bankers' and lived at Skinner Street, Snow Hill, London. Tried on four counts at the Old Bailey in front of Mr Justice Park on 12 April 1824, he was found guilty on the second count and sentenced to death.

Wagstaff was twenty-seven years old when tried, born on 30 April 1796 in Kidderminster, Worcestershire and is described in the Newgate Register as 5ft 8in tall, with a dark complexion, brown hair, hazel eyes, and 'stoutish'. Many petitions were sent following his conviction, supporting his claims that he was the victim of a dishonest London agent and his wife, young child, sisters and aged parents were dependent upon him. He was the only son of a former miller who had been forced to change trades and become a carpet manufacturer but knowing nothing about the business he was dependent on others. According to a letter sent by 'a distant relative', M.D. Hill, to George Marriott, a friend of Mr Justice Park, the 'London agent in a short time absconded with property to the amount of many thousand pounds'. John Hill Wagstaff's father sent his son to London although he was only sixteen years old and, Hill later explains:

'To escape the embarrassments occasioned by their heavy loss, they fell into the snare of drawing and accepting accommodation bills and by false credit thus obtained, they went on for several years with apparent success and I believe were weak enough to consider their prosperity real.'

Over time, the Wagstaffs' bills acquired a bad reputation and, forced to look for other means of finance, they 'entered into various speculaties, all of them doubtful, some of them desperate, and some I fear of even a worse character.' Eventually, they were declared bankrupt and their creditors discovered the true state of affairs; the books were in a 'state of confusion' which the letter writer believes was because Wagstaff had spent all the time propping up day to day payments and not paying enough attention to their clerks.

When Wagstaff was taken in to custody, a small bottle of oxalic acid was found on him,[1] according the Old Bailey trial account. Wagstaff had a ready explanation, and an article from *Bell's Weekly Messenger* at hand which explained it could be used in making punch. But oxalic acid could also be used in detecting forged cheques – and for committing suicide. Aware of its latter use, the bottle was taken from him so that he did not poison himself. This would be the act of **John Burgh Montgomery**, alias **Colonel Wallace**, alias **Colonel Morgan**, convicted at the Old Bailey in May 1828 of uttering forged notes in September 1827. On the morning Montgomery was due to be executed, he was found dead in his cell, having consumed acid which was thought to have been passed to him inside Newgate gaol.

The petitions supporting John Hill Wagstaff were unsuccessful and he was executed on 1 June 1824.

William Collier was tried at the Old Bailey, January 1834, on twenty counts relating to what the Home Office petition file notes describe as 'Aiding to personate for the purpose of transferring stocks'. Found guilty, with a recommendation from the jury of mercy because of previous good character, Collier was sentenced to transportation for life.

44-year-old Collier was a surgeon, then wholesale druggist, who was married with eight (or nine) children. Originally from Stokenchurch, Oxfordshire, he had resided in Liverpool but possibly now lived near Henley-On-Thames, Oxfordshire. Despite his claims that he had had no intention to defraud, and petitions from his wife, Sarah, and local supporters, Collier was ordered to the *York* hulk. Although his behaviour on the hulk was 'good' he was transported to Van Diemen's Land from Portsmouth on the *Arab*'s second transportation sailing, arriving in June 1834.

When he arrived at Hobart Town, information within the Home Office file shows he became a medical attendant at Bridgewater. Tasmanian archives show Collier was recommended for a Conditional Pardon in June 1845, which appears to have been approved the following year.

Edward Barr was a solicitor in his mid-thirties from Leeds, found guilty at York Lent Assizes in 1836 of defrauding County Funds. He had forged four payment orders totalling around £1,400 and received a severe sentence of one year's imprisonment with hard labour, followed by transportation for life.

Barr was part of a very respectable family, with good connections, as was his wife, Maria, with whom he had four children, the youngest born five months after Barr was taken in to custody. Petitions of support were sent to the Home Secretary from 178 local people, including the Mayor of Leeds and magistrates; this support would continue throughout Barr's imprisonment and years as a convict in Australia. Some weeks after Barr's imprisonment, his wife and brother tried to reimburse the county for the money Barr had taken. Maria Barr was wealthy and Barr's brother Robert was clerk to the Justices and principal partner in the firm of Barr, Lofthouse & Nelson, solicitors. However, their money was returned after a county meeting unanimously agreed that acceptance would have punished the family; Edward Barr was already paying the price.

Barr suffered ill health whilst in gaol, but his good behaviour throughout and the support for his case received by the Home Office, did not prevent him being sent to Sydney on the *Lloyds* in the spring of 1837.

During the journey, on 9 May, Barr was put on the sick-list but discharged four days later, suffering from 'constipation, dyspepsia' according to the surgeon's log. The following month another entry shows a cut finger on 10 June became troublesome:

> 'A simple incised wound which was first treated with adhesive plaster, it subsequently became very unhealthy looking and poultices were used.'

He was discharged from the sick list on 28 June 1837.

A letter from Dr Thomas McChristie supporting a large petition tells how Edward had taken with him to New South Wales:

> '... besides many letters from highly respectable persons (including Lord Morpeth) on the subject of his case, and expressive of the deepest sympathy on the part of the Writers for his condition and the unhappy state of mind of his innocent and suffering Wife and Children, letters from the Honble William Lascelles (Earl Harwoods Son) and Mr Baines, MP for Leeds, addressed to the Governor of Sydney certifying most highly in favour of his character in all aspects of his committing the forgery, and earnestly recommending him to the indulgent notice of the Governor ... Through the Surgeon having been assured of his good character; and from what he had learnt of him and his family having been induced to feel deeply for his misfortune he separated him from the other convicts and took him out as his Clerk....'

Barr then had introductions to 'several respectable Houses in Sydney' and the family's aim was to ensure he was allowed to remain there or be returned to Sydney if he had been sent elsewhere.

Edward Barr was sent to Port MacQuarie where he was employed as a confidential clerk to Major Innes and also employed by A. James. Annotations on his Home Office case notes show that in February 1842 his sentence was reduced to fourteen years. He was granted a ticket of leave in April 1843 and received an Absolute Pardon following a letter from the Colonial Office of November 1846.

George Forbes Atkinson was sentenced to transportation for life after being found guilty of forgery at the Old Bailey, in January 1837. The 39-year-old former captain of the 40th Regiment of Foot was accused on six counts concerned with the forging of a bill and intending to defraud Captain

Lauderdale Maule and others. Captain Lauderdale Maule was in the 79th Highland Regiment and a son of Lord Panmure, William Ramsay Maule, who had been an MP and entered the House of Lords in 1831.

George Forbes Atkinson petitioned the Home Secretary four times and his wife, Frances, (also known as Fanny), petitioned at least eight times in the following seven years. Details show he was respectably connected; his brother-in-law was Charles Hare, Director of Divinity, Fellow of Dublin College, and his brother was Receiver General at the Post Office in Dublin, appointed, Atkinson stated, by the Marquis of Anglesey. Atkinson himself had been in the Navy before joining the 40th Regiment of Foot, where he claimed he carried the colours at the Battle of Waterloo. With regard to his conviction, Atkinson told how he had been afflicted with 'brain fever' but maintained he was innocent of the crime of which he had been accused; he had not been directly involved but he implicated in the forgery the Honourable Mr Ashley, the youngest son of the Earl of Shaftesbury. He claimed he had two witnesses who saw Mr Ashley make the alteration. The Home Office annotation shows that, whether or not Atkinson's claims were believed, it was thought better that he was kept at a distance. It states:

'Write to Governor of New South Wales to watch his conduct and recommend him if he behaves well – but not to return to this country.'

From the *Justitia* hulk, Atkinson was transported to Van Diemen's Land on the *Blenheim* in March 1837. From a Home Office annotation it appears that Atkinson's wife joined him in January 1843. Tasmanian archives show he was recommended for a pardon in 1845, received it in 1846, and died of an abscess three years later, his age given as fifty-three, in Hobart.

John Hill Wagstaff, William Collier, Edward Barr and George Forbes Atkinson had all been found guilty of forging orders, bills or transfers but the forging and passing of notes of money was also a common crime.

If **Josiah Cadman** and Sarah Fone had hopes for years of companionship and mutual support when they married in April 1819[2], their wishes were short lived. On 15 September 1821, less than two and a half years after their wedding in Cobham, Kent, the Cadmans were facing separate trials at the Old Bailey, charged with uttering false bank notes. They both pleaded guilty and both were sentenced to death.

27-year-old **Sarah Cadman** had been taken in to custody in late July 1821. She is described in the Newgate Register of Prisoners as 5ft 6in tall, with a dark complexion, brown hair, grey eyes and 'stout made' and being charged with 'disposing of and putting away two forged £5 notes with intent to defraud the Governor and Company of the Bank of England' on 29 June[3]. Her status is 'married' and her birth place, Chatham in Kent. She had given her name as 'Ann Smith' and would later say this was to protect her husband.

At the end of the following month, on 30 August, Josiah Cadman was taken in to custody, charged with the same offence as his wife, save for uttering a single £5 note which he had tried to pass on 7 July. According to the Newgate Register of Prisoners he was 5ft 7in tall, with a dark complexion, brown hair, grey eyes and 'slim made'. His birth place is given as Atherton, Warwickshire and his age as twenty-six.

The case of the Cadmans drew much attention. An anonymous petition, addressed to the Duke of York, made its way to Viscount Sidmouth, the Home Secretary with an unidentified newspaper clipping attached which described the sentencing of the couple. The newspaper claimed Josiah Cadman was 'overpowered with grief' when the Clerk of the Arraigns asked if he had any comment to make as to why he should not receive the sentence that awaited him; he could only say he hoped his wife's life would be spared. When Sarah Cadman was asked the same question, she replied only that if her husband was to be executed she hoped she would share the same fate. The article recounted the event was 'truly distressing' and most of the people there, particularly the women, 'were quite overcome.' In this report, Cadman's age is given as thirty-four, and Sarah's as twenty-seven. According to the paper, Sarah 'appears to be a woman of superior address and education'. *Trewman's Exeter Flying Post* and other papers[4] wrote of her being a 'young woman of respectable appearance'.

An undated petition was sent from seventy-one local people from Clerkenwell and the surrounding area. It requested mercy and transportation, and wrote of Josiah Cadman that he was 'Honest and industrious'. The petition is marked 'Nil'.

A plea for mercy was sent to the Home Secretary by a more indirect route. On 9 October 1821, a letter was sent from Boyne House in Tunbridge Wells, Kent, to Lady Blackwood. The writer, Henrietta Erskine, was familiar with the Cadmans' case from newspaper reports and asked Lady Blackwood to intervene 'knowing your intimacy with Lord Sidmouth'. The letter is within the Cadmans' petition file but there is no Home Office annotation upon it.

In an undated petition to the king sent from Newgate prison, on behalf of himself and his wife, Josiah Cadman explained the couple had 'declined taking up the time of the Court with their trials… humbly relying upon the hope of Royal Mercy'. They also hoped for leniency from the prosecutor, the Bank of England, as several people had received this before. The petition described how Josiah Cadman had done everything he could to right his wrong, by giving the Bank full details of his crime and of the pernicious practice that would, he suggests, lead to 'the hidden authors of it'. In addition, he had numerous supporting petitions and fulsome references to attest to his character.

Cadman outlined his background to show his respectability, and here stated his age as twenty-eight. He had served in the Royal Marines for more than six years and was well regarded by his superior officers. He was 'on the American station' under the command of Sir John Borlase Warren and had been involved in the attack upon Norfolk and the taking of Hampton, had been employed in blockading the Chesapeake for five months and spent a similar amount of time cruising off New York. However, in 1814 he was badly wounded in the chest whilst on board one of the boats 'cutting out the American Schooner *General Armstrong* in Fayal Roads…' After he had recovered from the injury, Cadman went to Jamaica and on to New Orleans where he served under Captain Kneeshaw on the *Censor* gun-brig. On returning to England he was employed in the in the Quarter Master's office at the Barracks at Chatham.

Cadman saved a small amount of money and procured his discharge from the Marines. He married Sarah on 5 April 1819, with the parish register of Cobham, Kent, stating they were both from that parish. The ceremony was conducted by vicar, John Stokes and witnessed by Mary Ann Peale and William Thiles. The couple then moved to London with the intention of starting a business, but this was not as easy as they had hoped and their money soon ran out. In a change of plan, Cadman found employment as a clerk in the office of an attorney, Mr Cook, of Woodbridge House, Clerkenwell. However, when he saw an opportunity to obtain a lease on a public house, which he thought would be a good business, his attempts to obtain it took up so much of his time that he had to give up his job with Mr Cook. He left that employment in January 1821 but the expected lease did not materialise, leaving him with no job but 'burdened with debts unavoidably contracted'. At the same time, Sarah Cadman became ill and needed medical attention and 'expensive nourishment when your wretched petitioner had not the means of procuring her the common necessities of life…' Cadman could not bear Sarah's distress, she who was 'dearer to him than himself' and 'in an evil hour' he succumbed and turned to crime to relieve their predicament.

Cadman made a very personal plea to the king:

> 'That debased as your petitioner is by the consequences of his crime the situation of his wife is the heaviest part of the weight which presses him down. Every honourable sentiment to which he could once justly lay claim. Every manly feeling which even his present degradation cannot deprive him of adds to the reproach of having by his pernicious counsel and example induced his wife to join him in a practice which her education, her Principles and her previous conduct have taught her to reject with horror.'

Having told the Bank of England all he knew about bank note forgery and the people involved, Cadman and his wife had been shocked to find the Bank pressed charges against them.

Whilst Cadman was in Newgate awaiting his trial, a petition had been sent from the Royal Marine Barracks, Chatham, dated 16 September and signed by twenty-three army people. Cadman's good conduct in the Chatham Division of the Royal Marines was confirmed by a certificate signed by four superior officers and dated 10 September 1821. In it William Bate, Adjutant, stated Cadman had served as a corporal and private from 16 January 1813-5 May 1819 and was discharged by purchase. Cadman's good conduct had led to him being recommended to William Bate, which in turn led to Cadman's role as clerk to Lieutenant and Quarter Master Payne. Lieutenant S.J. Payne confirmed that Cadman had been promoted to Corporal in February 1817 and added 'I always considered him a very honest steady and trustworthy young man'. Thomas Mould and Captain J. Kneeshaw were equally supportive. A favourable letter was sent to the Home Office on 13 November by Sheriff William Venables, forwarding these certificates, or copies of them. Venables also confirmed that the prisoners had behaved well whilst imprisoned in Newgate.

William Cook petitioned for mercy for his former clerk, in September 1821, confirming Cadman had worked for him from 1807-11 before he joined the Marines and again in 1819. Cook was unfaltering in his support which appears to have been sent to the trial Judge:

> 'I firmly believe that nothing but the most extreme distress and the starvation of his wife whose character was previously as respectable as his own could have induced him to commit the crime for which he has been sentenced.'

On 29 September, the Judge, Baron Graham, replied to Cook confirming his petition would be presented to the Home Secretary and expressing support for mercy for the prisoners.

On 28 October, Cadman petitioned Viscount Sidmouth from the condemned cells in Newgate. He explained again how the broken promise of a lease on a public house lead the Cadmans to be penniless and with no immediate hope of alleviating the situation. He claimed if he had been alone, he would have been able withstand this, having been used to hardship when he was in the army, but Sarah had become sick. He was in no position to be able to supply the couple with everyday necessities yet alone the good food and medical assistance she required. He described again how he was drawn to crime:

> 'At this unfortunate period when my mind was weakened by despair, and the contemplation of an affectionate wife pining for want of nourishment, and my body tortured by the pangs of famine, the fatal means of relief were presented to me in the crime for which I am sentenced. I embraced them, and forfeited my life and respectability at one stroke. To render my situation all more dreadful my wife the partner of misery is the sharer of my guilt and my sentence.'

He emphasised how he told the Bank of England everything he knew and 'petitioned to be allowed to plead guilty to the minor offence, but found to my utter dismay that the Bank Directors had resolved not to interfere.' He pleaded 'Guilty', with his fate in the hands of the prosecution. He asked that both he and Sarah be given the opportunity to 'turn the small abilities we possess to a useful and worthy purpose'. He pointed out there had been many recent cases where the offenders had lesser justification for their actions than that of he and his wife but 'in whose persons it has been considered that the ends of public Justice have been answered by their being transported …' Cadman stated that the judge, 'appeared … to be penetrated with the misery of my situation and promised to add his recommendation to my own prayer for Mercy!'

On 13 November Cadman petitioned again via Sheriff Venables, declaring 'I am not hackneyed in the practice for which I am condemned …' and he had been soon caught:

> 'I made the most ample disclosure in my power to the officers of the Bank of England who at the same time that they told me the Directors would make no promise said that as I was in the hands of honourable gentlemen I might hope for the best.'

But the Bank, he said, had adopted a new regulation.

A petition, character certificates and the judge's reply to William Cook were forwarded to the Home Secretary in a covering, favourable letter from James Bacon on 13 November. It is possible that the petition enclosed was that written by Cadman on 13 November.

As the Home Office annotation makes clear, both Cadman cases were 'Considered at Report in Council 15 Nov 1821'. There were twenty-one cases from the September Sessions and two from the February Sessions. The report to the King[5] was prepared by John Silvester, the Recorder of London, and includes those capitally convicted of burglary, highway robbery, stealing in a dwelling house, housebreaking, sheep stealing, cutting and stabbing, and uttering forged notes.

Of those from the September Session found guilty of uttering forged notes, Ann Smith (Sarah Cadman's alias), Ann Davis, Matthew Carr and 16-year-old William Brown had their sentences commuted to transportation for life. Against Josiah Cadman however was written, 'The law to take its course'. This was also the fate of **George Ellis**, (the alias of **John Martin Latkow**), **Thomas Topley** and **Edward Sparrow**, whose petitions were all unsuccessful, despite Latkow being the son of a solicitor of Doctor's Commons and petitions being sent on his behalf by prominent bankers and merchants.

William Cook, Cadman's former employer, led another petition on Cadman's behalf, reiterating that Cadman had only committed 'so nefarious and vicious a practice' as a means of saving his wife's life. The petition stated:

'That the Bank of England has for a great length of time pursued the uniform practice of allowing Prisoners in the situation of the object of this petition to plead guilty to the minor offence, having forged notes in their possession and suffering sentence of transportation to be passed thereon and have therefore expressed an opinion of the severity of the laws in this respect which cannot have failed to make a great impression on the public mind.'

It continued that Cadman's case was 'by no means as heinous as that of many persons who have profited by this indulgence…' and Cadman had done 'all in this power to repair the injury.' It ended by citing discrepancy:

'… and that it is as inconsistent with justice … that this criminal should suffer death for a crime of much less magnitude than those of others to whom the boon we now implore has been granted.'

Undated, though possibly written after Cadman's fate had been sealed, it is undersigned by fifteen supporters, including Cook.

The Times newspaper of Saturday 17 November 1821 gave an account of the Recorder's report made the previous Thursday and named those facing execution the following Wednesday. It described the men's reaction on being told the news by the Reverend Mr Cotton, Mr Baker and Mr Brown Junior on the evening the decision was made and claimed Cadman had immediately asked about Sarah's fate. When he was assured that she had received mercy, it was reported he said he could die happy. *The Times* reminded its readers that both Josiah and Sarah Cadman had pleaded guilty, promising to give the Bank of England full information. It mentioned Cadman's previous good character and conduct and how the Judge, Baron Graham, had considered the case deserving of Royal Clemency. The paper commented that the Bank of England appeared to have changed its established policy of sparing lives in Cadman's case.

Sarah Cadman petitioned three times. On 10 November, she had asked that both her and her husband's life be saved. By 17 November, she had received the news that her own life would be spared and, still in Newgate, she petitioned the king to spare that of her husband, beginning her letter, 'The heartbroken distracted humble penitent…' and referring to Cadman as:

> '… a beloved affectionate husband whose guilt was occasioned by sickness and distress and whose only hope is in your Majesty's well known lenient mercy to the truly penitent and distressed and Oh if dared to trace the story of her hopeless woes Your Gracious Royall Heart would feel for her accumulating sufferings and hapless distiny… and spare Oh spare my beloved and truly penitent partner…'

She expressed her 'unbounded gratitude' to the king for sparing 'my wretched existence' and appealed to him:

> 'to finish the good works and bind up the wounds of the wretched by restoring to her her tender and beloved partner and Oh may your Majesty's Gracious Royall Mercy forbid my widow'd tears to flow with a fervent penitent contrition for my offence…'

She wrote to the king again on 19 November, her even greater distress apparent.

On the same day, Monday 19 November, two days before Cadman's execution, *The Times* showed its support for Cadman's case clearly briefed by Cadman's supporters. Under the heading, 'CASE OF CADMAN – (From a Correspondent)' it noted Cadman was only young and not a career criminal. Reiterating details of his previous good character, service record and employment history, the paper stated it had seen 'certificates' to this extent which were being forwarded to the Home Secretary, adding that whilst Cadman worked for the solicitor in Clerkenwell, he was noted for his industry and punctuality. It was only when his wife became ill and Cadman needed money that, as a temporary measure, he passed forged notes supplied by a coffee-shop keeper in Drury Lane. They claimed he had only passed notes twice before he was caught and, once he was imprisoned, he volunteered all he knew about 'the nefarious traffic' to the Bank of England. The Bank in England had apparently indicated Cadman should hope for the best as he was dealing with 'honourable Gentlemen'.

On the day before the execution, 20 November 1821, a second anonymous petition was sent to the Home Secretary. The writer claimed never to have met Josiah Cadman but had read the reports in the paper. It urged the reader, 'Think on this. That mercy I to others shew/That mercy shew to me.' The letter referred to the 'heavy obligations we are under as Christians' who are commanded to '<u>love one another</u>'.

An anonymous letter had been sent to Horse Guards and was forwarded to the Home Office by the Commander-in-Chief there, but it is unclear whether this is a third unsigned letter (which is not in the Home Office file), or one of the previous two anonymous letters received.

The Times of Thursday, 22 November 1821 reported on the last hours of the condemned men, detailing how they had been visited by friends during Tuesday. They remarked the meeting between Josiah and Sarah Cadman was of even greater interest because she had been found guilty but her life had been spared. It described how, for Sarah, the meeting consisted of repeated embraces but her husband had talked vigorously of his faith 'in a future state' due to his sincere contrition. The couple had embraced for longer than the time usually allowed and Cadman 'tore himself from her arms' with much difficulty. The press room had been told by the Ordinary who witnessed the Cadmans' parting that Sarah Cadman was 'maniac' describing her eyes as bulging as she pulled at her hair.

Shortly after 7 o'clock, the Sheriffs arrived and those in the press-room heard the death bell sound from half past the hour. The Reverend Cotton led the prisoners in to the room. The report stated that it was mentioned in the press-room that Cadman had considered he still might obtain a reprieve until the last moment, but noted that wasn't their impression when he had his irons struck off. Cadman reportedly thanked the Sheriffs, and his friends for their attempts to save his life and their kindness; he said he hoped he would be the last to die for this offence. He also told the onlookers they would be shocked if they knew how easy it was to procure forged notes. The report recounted how someone in the huge crowd shouted 'murder' when Josiah Cadman appeared on the platform amidst other groans and cries of support.

The newspaper carried 'Another Account – (From a Correspondent)' who gave similar details of the process before the execution, then added that Cadman was the first man to be summoned and calmly climbed the scaffold. He spoke to the crowd when the noose was around his neck saying he hoped what they were watching would deter them from giving in to the same temptation and thus disgrace. After all the men had come on to the scaffold, Cadman addressed the crowd saying he died 'in peace with all men …' that he loved his wife, the king, his country and God. His last speech was published in several broadsheets.

Below the report is a comment from a 'highly respectable correspondent' remarking that Cadman would have been resigned to his fate but was bitter he had not been shown the leniency afforded to well-known and worse offenders. It also commented upon public opinion regarding the large number of hangings.

By 24 November 1821, the tone of *The Times* had changed towards Josiah Cadman. The paper noted there had been so much 'conversation' about the executions of Cadman and Ellis and stated it was glad to be returning to the subject to give its own opinion. The article pointed out the earlier correspondent had wanted to see less capital punishment and, whilst the paper generally agreed, if all it had heard about Cadman was true, then he deserved his fate. Information had come to them which showed Cadman was not a mere utterer of forged notes, but a dealer. The paper believed that he had thus caused the deaths of others to whom he had sold the forged notes and if this was true it considered him a cold and harsh murderer who deserved to be hanged. It acknowledged Sarah Cadman's grief and respected her remorse but the paper's sympathy would increase if it was sure she was grieving for the loss of other lives as well as that of Josiah Cadman. The paper commented that Sarah Cadman's case strengthened the case for the abolition of capital punishment.

On 10 December, under 'News In Brief', *The Times* that reported 'Cadman's wife' was still in Newgate prison and attributed this report to the *Kentish Gazette*.

Josiah was a young man of 'no common attainments', according to the *Leeds Mercury* newspaper, reporting three days after his execution. He had written many dramatic pieces, amongst which was *The Father's Curse* performed in 1820 at Sadler's Wells which was well-received, and had translated *D'Auglade* from the French. It was noted however that although he had been engaged at Sadler's Wells to write 'pieces for representation' he did not 'pay that attention the theatre required.' There were reports of an expected inheritance of £20,000 he would be sharing with just one relative. *The Times*, in its report of the parting of Cadman and his wife on the day of his execution also understood Cadman had been employed to write pieces for Sadler's Wells Theatre: 'Some little productions, which were generally attributed to him … became popular; but his habits were dissipated …' Cadman's fluidity with words, used in the theatre, would later be seen in his eloquent address from the gallows, and the many letters and petitions which remain.

On 23 August 1822, Sarah Cadman was moved to the *Lord Sidmouth* at Woolwich.[6] The following month the ship set sail via Hobart to Sydney, arriving there in February 1823. New South Wales Archives suggest Sarah Cadman, (under the names of Ann Smith and also it seems Ann Cadman), asked for permission to marry the following year, and became the wife of James Hindhaugh, who had been convicted at Newcastle upon Tyne in 1818 and travelled on the *Baring* transport shop. He was born in 1798.

Working as an upholsterer, Sarah Cadman obtained a ticket of leave and received a conditional pardon in February 1843.

Letters of **William Hay, (James Hay)** sent from the *York* hulk, appeared in Chapter 3. His background and the details of the crime he committed add more context to those letters and his comments therein.

Unemployed and starving, William (alias James) Hay could not believe his luck when he passed through Fleet market, London, and saw papers under a butcher's block which on closer examination he found to be money. This, he claimed was how he came to be in possession of, and spend, forged notes, which lead him to be tried at the Old Bailey December Sessions 1823, and sentenced to death.

William Hay was a printer, stationer and bookseller. Born in Madras, he referred to himself as the natural son of the brother-in-law of the Earl of Dalhousie. (The Earl of Dalhousie was the uncle of Lauderdale Maule, the alleged intended victim of George Forbes Atkinson, whose crime and punishment appears earlier in this chapter.) William Hay's father was James Hay, who had married Lady Mary Ramsay, the Earl of Dalhousie's sister, on

18 April 1801 and the couple had twelve children. James Hay was the proprietor of Collipriest House in Tiverton, described by John Preston Neale in Volume 2 of Jones's *Views of the Seats ... of Noblemen and Gentlemen in England, Wales, Scotland and Ireland* as a 'Mansion' and Hay had 'raised the edifice a story and has made many additions and great improvements in the pleasure grounds and plantations around'. William Hay's age is given as twenty-six at the time of his trial in 1823, and by his use of the term 'natural' son, it would seem he was not the son of Lady Mary. This would account for his lack of familial support and impecunious situation. He was taken to Newgate on 5 November 1823, and the Newgate Register of Prisoners describes him as twenty-six years old, 5ft 5in tall with a dark complexion, auburn haired with grey eyes and 'stoutish'.

At his trial at the Old Bailey, on 6 December 1823, in front of Mr Justice Bailey, Hay was found guilty of uttering a forged Bank of England £5 note. According to the account of the Old Bailey Proceedings[7] the crime had taken place on 27 October at St Marylebone when Hay had tried to pass a forged note to Samuel Minton. Minton was a woollen draper from The Minories in the City of London and Hay had been one his customers for the last six years. However, Hay had been indebted to Minton for almost five years, owing him £3 18s 3d, and on 27 October, Hay told Minton that he had come to pay off part of the debt. Minton told the judge he had seen Hay only once in the last four years and had not pressed the issue of the debt feeling it would be of no use, due to Hay's 'distressed circumstances'.

Minton had shown the note to his neighbour, Isaac Johnson, a linen draper also living in The Minories and the police were sent for. Hay had remained in Minton's shop whilst Minton had gone to Johnson and was then apprehended by James Roberts, a City police officer.

Roberts told the court that Hay had claimed the note had come from his father, 'a very respectable man at Tiverton, in Devonshire', via a man in a public house in the Old Bailey. The prisoner's former landlady, Mary Flook, confirmed that he had lodged with her until around eighteen months before in Middle Street, Cloth Fair, but she did not know his current address. Unfortunately, Flook's was the address Hay had offered Issac Johnson when his suspicions were raised regarding the note.

Sarah Mills, the daughter of Matthew Mills of the Red Cow public house in Long Lane, said she had seen the prisoner five days prior to his visit to Minton. She had known Hay for between four and five years, but had not seen him for over a year and a half, although he had been to their house. Hay had an outstanding debt with them of 4s 9d and on 22 October came to pay the debt in full, offering a £5 note. Sarah's mother had remarked on the unclear water-mark but Hay had told them it was a note from his father and wrote J. Hay, Tiverton on it. Sarah had given him the change, then, when she heard the note was forged, had given it to William Bennett.

Hay had an outstanding debt of £2 8s 6d with William Bennett, a publican of Charterhouse Lane. Around two or three days before he went to the Mills', he visited Bennett, who had known him for about a year, and paid off part of his debt. Hay used a £5 note which Bennett had later paid to a tax-gatherer by the name of Sainsbury. The following week, Hay came to Bennett again and paid off more of his debt, again using a £5 note which he said was from his father in Tiverton. Hay told Bennett that he was going away to the country for a fortnight but would return afterwards to clear more of his debt. The trail of notes was followed through various witnesses as each could vouch for its passage or had written from whom they'd received it, and when, on the note itself.

Other witnesses gave details of Hay's recent background. Letitia Beckett, the wife of the publican of The Bells in Church Row, Aldgate, confirmed Hay had lodged with them for three or four months, leaving around five or six months before. She told the court that at that time he was working at an engraver's in Aldgate and off-set part of his debt to the Becketts by printing some cards for them. About ten days before he was apprehended, Hay had visited them to clear his debt, telling Letitia Beckett he had not found work but that he had received money from his father in Tiverton. Again, he used a £5 note and gave them the Middle Street address.

Speaking in support of the prisoner, Thomas Charles Lewis, a printer from The Minories, said that he had been the prisoner's Master, and Hay was the natural son of James Hay of Collipriest House, Tiverton. Hay had come to Lewis as an apprentice through one of Lewis's friends but had left him in 1818. Although Lewis had written to James Hay, and he to Lewis, the two men had never met.

John (or James) Bennell, of Copthall Court in the City, was James Hay's solicitor and had been so for about three years. In April 1822, James Hay had gone to the East Indies and died in Calcutta on 12 October that year, at the age of fifty-two.[8] Bennell settled his affairs and now acted for his widow, Lady Mary Hay, who had not gone abroad with her husband.

An inspector of bank notes and a cashier at the Bank of England both confirmed the bank notes, shown in court, were forgeries.

William Hay gave a lengthy written defence, in which he explained long-term unemployment, ensuing debt and lack of support had reduced him to destitution with no lodgings. He applied to his parish, St Botolph's in Aldgate, but they would not give him relief, on the basis that he was a good young workman so should be able to find work. He reapplied several times, eventually receiving 2s, 1s and 2s over almost three months. He wrote to the Lord Mayor and tried to give him the letter at Mansion House but was turned away without being able to deliver it.

Without money, Hay had to walk the streets, often without food or sleep for days on end in all weathers, he wrote. His health and appearance worsened, making it even more difficult for him to find employment but he kept away from crime and tried to keep his spirits up with the hope of work in the future, as some masters had promised him. Then, one day, whilst walking through Fleet market, he saw paper under a butcher's block which turned out to be bank notes. He went first to the people to whom he owed money, having no idea that the notes were forgeries. He appealed to the jury, saying that any person thinking the notes to be counterfeit would not pass them on to people who could later identify the source. Also, he would not have been so unfeeling as to give the notes to those who had shown him kindness and charity. Hay explained that, had his need been less desperate, he would have advertised the notes and given them back to whoever claimed them, but his needs were so great he transgressed. He was sure that he would be given good character references by those who knew him; mentally, he had suffered greatly.

Despite the excellent character references given by Minton, William Bennett, Beckett and Mills, Hay was found guilty and sentenced to death. The prosecutor and all the other witnesses recommended mercy, knowing the distressed state of the prisoner and that he was looking for work.

As a pre-emptive measure, on 20 January 1824, John Bennell wrote to Norman Knowles, the Recorder of London, stating, 'I believe you have not yet made your Report to His Majesty...' As Bennell was to relate in a later letter to John H. Capper, Superintendent of prisons and hulks, Bennell had not known William Hay prior to his trial but had been subpoenaed to be a witness against him. However, Bennell was 'struck ... forcibly' by the fact that Hay might have found the notes, a fact made more likely because Hay had tried to pay off his debts to people who could identify him. It was clear that Hay was 'literally starving' from his inability to find work despite his efforts and, as Hay had claimed, this was the reason he did not advertise the notes. This was Hay's first offence and the jury had recommended mercy. Ten days later Bennell wrote to the Recorder again, saying that he had also sent letters to the Lord Chancellor and Robert Peel, the Home Secretary.

Hay's case was considered at King in Council on 19 March 1824 and here his sentenced was reduced to transportation for Life.

Bennell wrote to Capper, on 29 March 1824. He explained his involvement and how Hay's father had been an honourable man. He told Capper that Hay was a printer:

> '... and is well known to the Relations of a Master Printer in Sidney who it is reported would be induced to employ him and make him a freeman of that Country.'

Bennell requested Hay be sent there and Hay would show his gratitude through his conduct. He also took the opportunity of mentioning the prisoner was the natural son of the brother-in-law of the Earl of Dalhousie. Hay was removed from Newgate on 5 May 1824 and taken to the *York* hulk ship at Gosport.

In early July, Bennell wrote to Robert Peel requesting Hay be sent on one of the next convict transport ships and added 'it would be doing an act of kindness which I really believe his good conduct would deserve.' He enclosed a letter from Hay pressing for the same. (See Chapter 3.)

Later that month, on 20 July 1824, Hay wrote to Capper outlining his situation. Seemingly admitting his guilt, he explained he was:

> '... lead astray through artifice of my enemies to expose myself to the just laws which I bitterly lament I have infringed and my being totally destitute of Relations since my Father's death in India about 18 months back.'

He states he believed his request to go to Sydney had been supported by Captain Lamb on the *York* hulk and looked upon favourably but nothing seemed to have happened. He wrote eloquently of the current conditions of his trade:

> 'Through the introduction of Machinery and Boys (my trade especially) there was very little opportunity for a regular journeyman to always find employment.'

Performing well in his work meant he was liked by employers but not always by his fellow journeymen workers, who 'universally combined to get me discharged... depriving me of getting a respectable and comfortable independent livelihood' and during a period of unemployment he 'unfortunately became acquainted with a young man' who through drink led him to attempt to pass a forged £5 note 'without reflecting on the awful danger I was exposing myself'.

Hay's letter expressed self-torment at his actions, though whether or not the words were merely for Capper's benefit, is uncertain:

'I feel sensibly awakened and I have experienced a multitude of griefs almost bordering at intervals upon derangement or temporal insanity.'

He assured Capper he intended to avoid being drawn in to bad company and, if allowed to go to Sydney:

'I hope Providence will mercifully bestow upon me an opportunity to return my sensible gratitude to your having crowned my endeavours with laurels of compassionate success.'

The letters in Chapter 3 show Hay's requests for Bennell's assistance in obtaining provisions on the hulk and his help to secure Hay's early transportation. Increasingly desperate, in his letter of 2 July 1824 Hay stated:

'I have not heard from any person but if I should not be sent by the next Ship I shall write to Lady Mary and the Hon John Ramsey to beg their charitable assistance to procure food…'

It seems clear that Lady Hay is not William Hay's mother but it's difficult to ascertain whether this comment was more menacing than it might at first appear.

William Hay was sent to Port Jackson on the *Asia* departing England in early January 1825. It is possible he was the convict James Hay, compositor, holding a ticket of leave, who was accused with two others of stealing and receiving a printed proof slip from the *Herald* newspaper in 1835. A report of the committal of 27 July 1835 appears in the *Sydney Morning Herald* under the heading 'The Conspiracy!!'. It recounts how the value of the proof slip was greatly debated, including whether it had any value at all. Hay had been working at the *Herald* but had been 'induced by higher wages' to join the *Gazette*. The report continued:

'This case excited great interest in Sydney; and at one time we noticed thirteen Magistrates on the Bench; and the body of the Court was literally crowded with spectators.'

The case was heard in August and all three men were found 'Not Guilty' in what appears might have been part of a bigger inter-paper conflict.

New South Wales Archives show that William (alias James) Hay received a Conditional Pardon on 1 February 1845.

Chapter 7

Words from Forgers on Forging

S ome prisoners leave us with information they may not have intended
the Authorities to obtain as in the case of **William Strang** (Chapters
3 and 4). Strang was found guilty of theft and his Home Office petition file contains papers taken from him whilst he was on board the *Justitia*
hulk at Woolwich in 1829. In these he describes how to make 'sham couters';
counterfeit coins.

Strang instructs the reader to gather together:

> 'Fine Copper, Yellow Bell metal, Gold, Two steel rings 2 inches in
> diameter, and ¾ of an inch in thickness both of them flattened a
> little on each side, A crucible, a small ladle, a Phial of Aqua Fortis, A
> tumbler of Pure Water, Fine Powdered chalk or whitening a saucer
> having a smooth edge three steel or iron pegs nearly ¾ of an inch in
> length tapered from the top to bottom and two or three spoonfuls
> of cream of tartarium.'

He urges the reader to 'take great care' when milling and handling the met-
als; if not, 'one false step will cause you much trouble and expense.'

In order to prepare the false coin for ringing, Strang writes there are
three processes to follow:

> 'Making of the Mould, the casing of the Couter and the Making
> and using of the Wash… for rubbing it with.'

To make the mould the saucer is put 'on a smooth board or table' and filled
with the powdered chalk which is then smoothed and pressed down. In to
this is placed a sovereign which has been previously smoked by heating
resin on brown paper 'because if you do not the metal will adhere to it'.
With a small diagram to illustrate his explanation of the following steps,
Strang explains the coin is pressed half down in the chalk and one of the
rings is placed around it; the three pegs are placed between the ring and
the coin.

Copper is melted in the crucible, using a low heat, then poured over the sovereign until the metal reaches the top of the ring. He continues:

> '… you then take up the half mould with the sovereign still adhering to it and take a fine tooth brush and sweep all the chalk from the Sovereign and Mould and take care not to disturb the couter.'

The sovereign and the mould are then blackened with the resin and brown paper. The second ring is placed on top of the first and, with the sovereign inside, the rings are filled with metal to the rim. After being allowed to cool the mould is given a 'good stroke' with the hammer to open it. The mould has to be blackened well before every Sovereign is cast but, Strang assures the reader, 'if you cast this mould well there will not be the least difference between the real ones and the Sham one' and urges repeated castings to ensure good quality:

> 'because it is much better for you to have a superior article for the better they are they will pass easier and sell higher 6 or 7 shillings you will get for each of them.'

Having given this detailed account of how to make the mould, Strang writes that he will move on to the next stage, 'the casting of the Sovereign'. However his note ends at this point, without the second step being explained. A separate note, repeating details from the first, urges the reader to cast a shilling or sixpence first then melt ball or pin metal and cast.

The third step of the process is described on the back of a letter to his parents, written whilst he was still on the *Justitia* hulk, but was perhaps only a draft, he had a change of mind or needed to put the paper to more immediate use. This step is 'the making and the washing the gold on the sovereign'. A small piece of 'real guinea gold about the size of a pea' is steeped for five minutes in 1½ tablespoonsful of Aqua Fortis in a cup. To this is added 'a tablespoonful of cream of tartar or rather Salt then it will begin to effervesce' resulting in the gold being 'reduced to a powder.' To the cup is added 'Cold Spring Water', the contents all stirred for around ten minutes and the excess water 'and other substances' are poured away to leave the gold in the cup. This process is repeated with salted water until the gold is purified and turned to 'dust'.

The gold dust is stirred with a glass stalk then allowed to stand for 'an hour or two' at which point it is stirred again until the gold is completely dry. A little of the dry gold is then rubbed over the sovereign with a wetted thumb. Strang notes that 'a very little of it will work one' and continues, 'the more you rub it and the more you put on it, the prettier will it look'. According to Strang, the pea-sized gold, if powdered well, will 'wash 2 or three hundred ...' and to prevent dust from mixing with the gold, he urges covering it after use. The instructions end here.

The information on coining only added to other reasons which would see Strang transported to New South Wales. As detailed in Chapter 3, his behaviour on board the hulks lead to the report from John H. Capper, that Strang's earliest transportation was advisable.

Robert Peel agreed and Strang was transported on the *Mermaid* in December 1829, arriving in New South Wales the following May.

Whilst Strang gave information about a process unwittingly, over two years earlier **James Boot** had given information about fellow forgers willingly, in an attempt to save his own life. He was convicted of Uttering at Warwick Assizes before Mr Justice Holroyd and sentenced to be executed on 14 April 1827. On 4 April, awaiting his fate in Warwick gaol, Boot gave information to the Under-Sheriff of Warwickshire, Mr Whately, who sent it in a letter to the High Sheriff, William Dilke, who in turn wrote to the Home Secretary, Robert Peel, on 6 April 1827.

Dilke informed Robert Peel he had sent a copy of the statement to Mr Freshfield, the Bank of England's solicitor, and notes 'several of the persons named are not even suspected by the Police of Birmingham.' He also informed the Home Secretary that Boot had offered 'to make this communication to the Bank through his solicitor before the Trial, and the Bank declined to receive it.'

On the same day, Freshfield & Son wrote to Spurrier & Ingleby, solicitors in Birmingham, enclosing Boot's statement as written by Under-Sheriff Whately. Freshfields request that Spurrier and Ingleby:

'... will be so good as inform us by Sunday's Post how far this statement can be considered as worthy of credit as to the principal individuals pointed out by Boot and how far is has the merit of being new.'

Freshfields state that they know of many of the people named and others are likely to be familiar to the Birmingham Police but they urge the use of considerable caution in enquiries of the police 'as we place very little confidence in their discretion'. They cast doubt on the short length of time Boot says that he has been involved in passing false money particularly as they understand he was in custody seventeen years ago for paying with a counterfeit coin. However, that Bill 'was ignored and no suspicion attached to him in respect to Bank Notes'. Indeed, the Warwick Archives shows that a James Boot appeared as case 14 in the Quarter Sessions, Easter Term, 1810, but he was 'discharged'.[1]

The following day, Spurrier & Ingleby replied to Freshfields and informed them that they had talked to 'the only person we have thought fit to entreat it to': policeman Redfern. From Redfern's information, the solicitors confirm Boot's lengthy involvement in forgery; he was a known dealer in forged Bank notes and counterfeit coins for almost twenty years. In addition, his name had been given as supplier by many people who had been convicted of uttering. The Birmingham police, they write, have long considered Boot 'to be the most extensive Dealer of forged notes and counterfeit coin in Birmingham'.

The solicitors give more details concerning Boot's previous brush with the law to which Freshfields referred, confirming Boot was implicated seventeen years ago with John Howell, Mrs Huxley, Joseph Jennens and others, all selling coin. All except Boot were taken at one time but after the others had been convicted, 'it was not thought worthwhile for Nadin of Manchester and Vickery and Armstrong of London and their witnesses to come such a distance again to give evidence against Boot.'

Spurrier & Ingleby tell how Boot briefly co-habited with Jennens wife, thirteen years ago, when Jennens was convicted and transported for having forged bank notes in his possession. They state that Boot omitted to mention this in his statement but acknowledge he did say it was through her that he first met Corbet:

> 'That may be true but he was a Dealer in Bank Notes years before then and has had several Presses for coin at work at different places near Birmingham, at which his Understrappers were employed, but not himself.'

Redfern had informed the solicitors that Boot was the supplier of forged notes to the well-known Mrs Smith of Bordesley Street and her associates. The solicitors note that Boot's information appears to be true but it holds no new details for the police; the only 'defective' element being that Boot has played down his own role over the last twenty years.

Spurrier & Ingleby had been informed that six years ago, Boot 'applied to a Man in this Town of the name of Johnson to sign notes for him.' Boot was named as the person who supplied notes by Grigg:

'convicted at Warwick in 1820 for selling forged notes … in fact he
was employed by Boot to deliver them and Boot was seen coming
down Grigg's stairs when the officers went to apprehend Grigg.'

The police found twenty-five forged bank notes in the pack of a saddle
in Grigg's chamber which, according to Grigg, had been left there by
Boot. Boot was also named by another man, Jones, who was convicted at
Worcester Summer Assizes in 1826 for uttering a £10 forged note and had
named Boot as his supplier. Indeed, when Jones was apprehended, his wife
was living at Boot's house.

In Boot's statement to the Under-Sheriff, he gives information on
many people but names Corbet and Ford as the two principal makers in
Birmingham. Joseph Corbet ran the Falstaff Public House in Hill Street,
Birmingham, and was an engraver by trade. According to Boot, Corbet
'engraves plates for Bank of England notes, casts the moulds for the letters
and figures and signs the notes.' Boot claimed Corbet made the plates for
William Booth who was executed at Stafford in August 1812. Booth had
forged notes, stamps and coins in the seclusion of his 200-acre farm in Perry
Barr.[2]

Boot claims to have seen Corbet sign notes in his parlour and that Corbet
has been making notes for at least ten years. He had met Corbet and his wife
around five years ago through Mrs Jennings or Jennens with whom Boot was
intimate. After their initial meeting, Boot had seen Corbet at Hartley's when
he lived in Summer Lane, but Hartley has moved to Liverpool 'and is doing
a great deal'. Later Corbet met Boot:

'… and asked him if he knew any of Mrs Jennings friends and said
he might have anything he wanted but it was a long time before he
had any dealings with him.'

According to Boot, Corbet makes plates for Morcus Fereday of Sedgley, and
they 'have many dealings together'. Fereday and Corbet made the watermark between them, purchasing the paper for their 'common things' from
London. Boot explains that 'common things' is paper with the watermark
pressed in. The watermark is pressed in in Birmingham.

Corbet procured the paper from Manchester for the 'best bottom', which
is paper with the watermark 'wore in'. It was delivered to Corbet by the
father and son who make it. Although Boot claimed never to have seen the
father at Corbet's, he had seen the son, who Corbet pointed out to him as

the person from whom he procured the paper. Boot described the son as being between 20 and 30 years of age 'about 5 foot 9 inches high and of plain appearance'. Although Boot once heard his name, he could not recall it.

Boot declared that the only person from whom he bought notes was Corbet, because his were the best. He claimed not to know where Corbet struck them off but he was aware that Corbet had a cottage at Northfield, which Boot had never visited. Corbet told Boot a short time before he was 'taken up' that:

'he had been very much alarmed for he had met Redfern the Police Officer who stopped and spoke to him in the street and he had at that time one of his Plates in his pocket'.

Boot told the Under-Sheriff that Corbet had the notes which were stolen from the Bolton Bank and 'Madden' was concerned in the Robbery. Corbet had asked Boot if he knew anyone who would 'put some off'. Corbet sold to Hartley, who was frequently at Corbet's, and Boot did not know how the notes are sent but he believed it was by a private hand.

Ford, of Carrs Lane, Birmingham, was a watchmaker 'who makes notes from the beginning' and worked closely with Manning 'who lives near the sign of the "Frightened Horse" at Handsworth and is a man of good address.' Ford employed Manning to put off stolen bankers notes or other property he received. According to Boot, the previous summer, Manning had told him:

'I could do you some good, old Jenny is at work again (meaning Ford). I have seen some of his things they are damned bad and I know his man. You may do something with him to do you good, he is very poor, and I can find out where he lives.'

Although Manning did not give Boot the man's name, he described him sufficiently enough for Boot to suspect that he knew who he was in a later encounter. About the same age and size as Boot, he was:

'dressed in a coat and waistcoat which he had seen Ford wear. He is dressed like a shabby gentleman and walks with a stick… and has returned from Transportation. He generally wears brown coat and grey waistcoat.'

Boot saw the man in the Handsworth Road and the man has passed his house 'several times… at the Five Ways …'

Left his Home

Yesterday Evening, between 6 & 7 o'clock,

A BOY

Between the age of Twelve and Thirteen Years; answers to the name of JOHN WISE.

Had on when he left home a Dark Brown Jacket, Corderoy Trowsers, and Blucher Boots. Any Information respecting him will be thankfully received at **21, Plough Court, Fetter Lane.**

APRIL 11th, 1837.

C. F. Seyfang, Printer, 57, Farringdon Street.

Handbill printed and circulated on the instruction of John Wise senior who was unaware his 12 year old son had been taken to the Station House and believed him to be missing. John Wise junior was convicted of theft in 1837. (See Chapter 4, Theft) *The National Archives UK*

Handbill offering a reward for the apprehension of 27-year-old John Hill Wagstaff. Wagstaff was later convicted of forgery at the Old Bailey, London, 1824, and sentenced to death. (See Chapter 6, Forgery) *The National Archives UK*

FORGERY,

100 Guineas REWARD.

WHEREAS

John Hill Wagstaff

LATE of Skinner Street, Snow Hill, in the City of London, Carpet Manufacturer, stands charged upon Oath with having committed divers Forgeries on several of the London Bankers; And whereas the said JOHN HILL WAGSTAFF has been Outlawed, for not surrendering to the Commission of Bankrupt issued against him, and has absconded;

THIS IS TO GIVE NOTICE, that the above Reward of ONE HUNDRED GUINEAS will be paid to any Person or Persons who will apprehend the said JOHN HILL WAGSTAFF, and lodge him in any of His Majesty's Goals, on application to Messrs. *Knight and Fyson*, Solicitors, No. 26 Basinghall Street, London.

DESCRIPTION.

The said JOHN HILL WAGSTAFF is about 5 Feet 7 or 8 Inches in height, stoops in the Shoulders, and carries his Head rather on one side; straight Black Hair, but no Whiskers; Dark Eyes, and keeps his Eyelids nearly closed; Complexion Dark, with a little Colour; has a weak Voice, and speaks deliberately ; Dresses plainly, and has a slovenly Walk or Gait. about 34 years of age.

EASTMAN, Printer, 100, Cheapside, London.

To the Right Honorable The Lord John Russell His Majestys Principle Secretary of State for the Home Department

The Humble Petition of Sarah George of Number Nineteen Little Wild Street Lincolns Inn Fields

Sheweth

That your Petitioner in approaching your Lordship does so with the deepest humiliation and respect

That your Petitioner is the Wife of Robert George a Prisoner now in His Majestys Goal of Newgate under sentence of Transportation for Life, having been convicted at the Session for the Old Bailey of ~~two~~ just terminated of stealing privately in the dwelling house of J. Simms property to the amount of Five pounds

That your Petitioners Husband up to the time of the Commission of this offence lived in the employ of One Master (Mr Barrow) for upwards of Four years during which period he bore a most exemplary character, and it is believed by all persons acquainted with him that this is his first offence

That upon the trial of the Prisoner it was proved that at the time of committing the offence the Prisoner was in great distress having your Petitioner and four small Children to support and many most respectable persons gave evidence to his former

(This page and opposite) Petition from Sarah George on behalf of her husband, Robert George. George, a carpenter, was tried at the Old Bailey, London, 1835, and found guilty of stealing a silver pendant rod and small sextant. (See Chapter 3, Words from the Hulks, and Chapter 4, Theft)
The National Archives UK

good conduct, and that the Prosecutor and Jury strongly recommended the Prisoner to Mercy

That your Petitioner is by no means ignorant of the great crime committed by her unfortunate Husband, but at the same time for the sake of herself and unfortunate children, she most earnestly implores your Lordship to cause inquiries to be made as to the truth of this Petition, and if upon such enquiries Mercy can with propriety be shewn the Prisoner by a mitigation your Petitioner most respectfully entreats your Lordship will recommend the same in the proper quarter.

And your Petitioner as in duty bound will ever pray &c.

We the undersigned having known the Prisoner George
for the number of years set opposite our respective
names, do, from his former good character, most
earnestly but respectfully beg leave to recommend
him to mercy—

William Simms. 136 Fleet Street, Prosecutor

John Barrow his Late Employer
   Nº 4 Salisbury Court Fleet Street
                                        4 years
A Francis Sun Tavern by 7 Long acre

Jeremiah Young 75 Castle St East,

John Wainscourse 24 Warwick Street

Fitzroy Square 9 years

Thomas Goode, 15 Mill Street, Hanover Square
   Landlord of House 19 Little Wild Street, occupied by the
   Prisoner, Robert George.   Little Wild Street

Mary Dean 4 Kings Head Yard, 4 years

William Burn 4 Kings Head Yard — 4 years

Jonathan Tibbs 24 Little Wild Street   2 years

   Thomas Fairbairn 19 Little Wild Str

John Parsons 11 Little Wild St, 4 years
                                 2 years
Thomas Blackford 20 Little Wild Street 3 years

Jonathan Jarvis 5 Little Wild St — 5 years

Charles Lacey 25 Little Wild St

Joseph James Smith 26 Little Wild Street

The *Warrior*,
Woolwich. In hulk
service from 1840.
*Illustrated London News –
The National Archives UK*

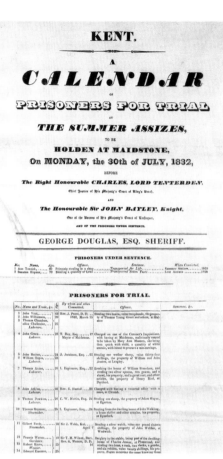

Calendar of Prisoners for trial,
Maidstone, Kent, 1832.

*Records of Justices of Assize, Gaol Delivery, Oyer and
Terminer, and Nisi Prius – The National Archives UK*

Postal Service 1837 illustration.

Copyright Office, Stationers' Company – The National Archives UK

Convicts rafting pine logs, Grummet Island, Macquarie Harbour, Van Diemen's Land, 1830.

Copyright Office, Stationers' Company – The National Archives UK

Convict Railway, Port Arthur, Van Diemen's Land, 1830.
Copyright Office, Stationers' Company – The National Archives UK

Convicts at work, Port Arthur, Van Diemen's Land, 1830s.
Copyright Office, Stationers' Company – The National Archives UK

Register of convicts on the
Antelope, Bermuda, 1823-28.
The National Archives UK

Royal Sussex Subscription
Theatre, Rip Van Winkle, 1833.
*Home Office, Ministry of Home Security,
and related bodies – The National
Archives UK*

Tolpuddle Martyrs cartoon, Dorchester Unionists imploring mercy of the King, 1834.
Home Office, Ministry of Home Security, and related bodies – The National Archives UK

Satirical cartoon of the police, 1833.
Home Office, Ministry of Home Security, and related bodies – The National Archives UK

Dec'r th 11 1832

to the Right Honerable

Lord Mellven

your humble pertinsher Catterane Day
in behafe of her unfortent son Robert Doy
was trid and convicked at horsmongger
sen esh and sentens for 14 yers Aged 12
yers hops your Lordshipn will plese to
pitty A power destressed widow Mother who is at
your Lordship marsey and is allmost in despar
if your Lordship will be plese to hepe him in this
Contrey on Counte of his tender yers to put him [in
to aney Asyulm your Lordship may think
propper hope your will parden your pertinsher
wrtch is at your Lordship marsey (as I dow not
know how to adrese my self to your Lordship powre
dressed Mother if your Lordship wold be plese
to malefy his time wrtch I am Duly Bound

ever to pray

Catterane Day

Petition from Catterane Day on behalf of her son, Robert Day, who was tried at Surrey Adjourned Quarter Sessions 1832 and found guilty of stealing a pair of boots. He was sentenced to 14 years transportation. *The National Archives UK*

Ford's son, Tom, travelled 'all over the country and goes to Fairs' selling notes for his father and Boot related how Ford senior showed Boot a bank note which was inside the family Bible; Ford senior had wanted Boot to 'deal with him' but Boot declined. Boot named Ford senior as having most of the stolen bank notes belonging to 'Taylor & Lloyds and of the Bank of Shrewsbury.' Ford also has a pattern for the Bolton Bank notes, according to a man of the name of Clement who lives near Bolton, Lancashire and dealt with the Smiths in Bordesley Street.

Edward and William Lane 'sell a great many notes and coin sovereigns and shillings and sixpences', dealt with Corbet and 'have a great many connections in Manchester'. Edward Lane had a house by the Chequers near 'The Bell' in the New Road, Birmingham, and William Lane in Park Street. According to Boot's statement 'the Lanes do more in a week than Boot did in a year'. Boot had all the sovereigns from the Lanes but says he never dealt with Maynard who had frequently asked him. The Lanes' things were better and that was the reason Boot dealt with them.

Although Boot claimed that he 'knew little of him', he named Benjamin Patrick who lives near Dromspare as a maker of bank notes. Patrick's brother Joseph, who formerly lived in Barr Street and now with him, was also a Dealer. James Phillips who lived near the 'Sailor's Return', Great Barr Street, was a Dealer and has been a maker; Mrs Jennings and Jim Woolley had their dealings with Corbet; Thomas Spooner the husband of Kit Spooner travelled and sold notes which he got from Corbet. Boot saw him there only a few days before he, Boot, was apprehended; Mrs Price who kept a worsted shop in Steelhouse Lane was also a seller of notes; John Maynard of Lawrence Street was a coiner and worked a press in the neighbourhood of Dudley or the Collieries.

Joseph Pring who lived with the Smiths, on Bordesley Street, was a seller and courier as was his son in law; Mrs Phillips of Tower Street dealt in notes but Boot did not know where she obtained them; John Lockit of Paice Street, victualler, used to sell notes for Lowe and also for Fereday of Sedgley. A man of the name of Parker sold for Lockit who lived close by.

When questioned, Boot declared that he did not know anything about Ashby but had no doubt he was murdered by the Moores and he thought it was confined to that family. He stated that Corbet was the principal man in England. Boot also declared that he never sold or gave to Whitehouse the notes which he swore to at the trial, but he did sell him the sovereigns.

On 9 April 1827, Freshfields wrote to Robert Peel, enclosing a copy of the reply 'their Agent' Spurrier and Ingleby had sent regarding their enquiries.

Freshfields added that they hoped their silence did not lead Peel to conclude they had no information to give:

> '... but for that consideration we should gladly relieve ourselves from any voluntary communication that may be prejudicial to the prisoner.'

Far from aiding his cause, Boot's information weighed against him. In a note from Peel to Henry Hobhouse, Under-Secretary of State at the Home Office, Peel writes, 'These seem conclusive against the Prisoner Boot.'

Boot was executed on 14 April 1827. According to a report in *The Cambrian* newspaper of Saturday 28 April 1827, he came from a very respectable family. Although his parents had 16 children, 'one of whom is now only alive viz. a sister, who attended him to his grave on the evening of his execution'. On the morning of the execution, Boot had:

> 'requested that a clean shirt might be well aired for him, and that he might be allowed to go to the place of execution with a silk handker-chief tied round his head, as he was so liable to take cold.'

John Grigg, who had named Boot as his supplier, had been convicted at Warwick Assizes on 27 March 1820, having forged Bank of England notes in his possession. He was sentenced to fourteen years transportation. Seven years later, at the age of forty, John Grigg appears on a recommendation list for the *Leviathan* hulk dated 30 June 1827, but his name is crossed out show-ing he did not receive any mitigation of sentence on this occasion. However, he is put forward on the *Leviathan's* recommendation list for the following quarter, dated 30 September 1827, and this time he appears to be more for-tunate. A free pardon was prepared for the successful prisoners in October 1827.

Chapter 8

Shooting and Stabbing with Intent

In the early nineteenth century, the rapid growth in Britain's population and its effects on society led to a change in how violence was viewed. Incidents once tolerated or managed inside small communities were felt to pose a greater, wider, threat when carried out by strangers in cities or within unpredictable large groups. By 1820, malicious shooting and stabbing was a capital offence and would remain so until 1837. The Home Office received many petitions relating to convictions on this charge. The circumstances which gave rise to the crime, and the victims of the assault, were wide-ranging.

William Hectrup, a shoemaker from Bishopsgate, London, was tried at the Old Bailey, in September 1830, accused of stabbing his wife Catherine. Found guilty, Hectrup was sentenced to death but this was commuted to transportation for life. In support of his plea for mitigation of his sentence, Hectrup claimed previous good character. Three petitions were sent from his victim, Catherine, a shoe-binder, in which she claimed she was to blame for her husband's actions: Catherine had told Hectrup she was carrying the child of a man with whom she'd been involved for over a year and Hectrup had been drinking when he heard her news. That Hectrup had only struck his wife once prior to this offence was put forward as a reason for mercy, along with the fact the wound for which he was tried was slight and Catherine was destitute. She was expecting her fourth child and, being Irish, had no claim for parochial relief. If Hectrup was transported, Catherine would poison herself with arsenic.

The Old Bailey Trial account[1] shows a different picture; they were a couple who did not live together and had a sparring but close relationship. Hectrup had been put in the comptor before because of a row with his young wife and although he was suspicious of Catherine's relationship with another man, Kelly, there is no mention of a pregnancy by him or anyone else. Witnesses agreed that Hectrup was not intoxicated at the time of the attack, although alcohol had been drunk, and Catherine's injuries kept her in hospital at least three days. Catherine refused to come to court, her later petitions saying she felt a prosecution was 'wholly unnecessary' and they demonstrate a desire to lessen the blame attributed to Hectrup, and to keep her husband from being sent abroad.

The petitions did not change Hectrup's fate. Tasmanian records show that he was transported to Van Diemen's Land, on the *Argyle*, in March 1831. Although the Old Bailey account notes his age as 38, Tasmanian records described him on arrival as 34 years old, 'stout made', 5ft 1¼in tall, with dark brown eyes, black hair and a dark complexion. His birthplace is given as Cashell, Ireland.

William Hectrup took his own life on 23 December 1844 in Carrick, Van Diemen's Land. The coroner's report states he hanged himself, 'not being of sound mind but labouring under a fit of temporary insanity...' It appears that his death is registered under the name of William Hectriff, shoe-maker.[2]

With conditions often challenging for those working at sea, it is not surprising that many petitions concern attacks on board ship, as in the case of **John Castle**, (or **Castles**) of Deptford, London. Castle was tried at the Old Bailey Admiralty Sessions, December 1823 and found guilty of stabbing, cutting and maiming Captain Clark, an East India man, on 30 March of that year. Sentenced to death, an execution date was fixed for 2 April 1824.

In the petitioning which followed sentencing, one of the reasons put forward for clemency was the cruel behaviour of Captain Clark towards his crew. Castle was successful and his sentence was commuted to transportation for life on 6 April 1824. Thirteen years later **Neil Thompson** was on the other side of a similar offence, charged with attempting to shoot with intent to murder a crew member.

Thompson was the mate on the brigatine *Heroine* when he was involved in an incident a mile and a half off the African coast, on 24 May 1836. In August of the following year he was tried at the Central Criminal Court, Old Bailey, and was convicted of assaulting Henry Kemp, (or Kempt), a seaman under his command, with the intent to do him bodily harm. Evidence came from the prosecutor, Kemp, and from two other shipmates, Mustard and Andrews. Unable to produce defence witnesses who could be present in England, Thompson was sentenced to death, (commuted to transportation for life.)

Whilst Thompson was in Newgate prison, his wife, Jane Thompson (or Thomson), petitioned the Recorder of London from her home in Newlands Field, Pollockshaws, Renfrewshire, Scotland. Writing on 21 August 1837, she described how the family had now been 'left in a distressed and heart breaking condition' and for her husband she begged:

> 'O do not my Lord send him out of his country (when he may be as he has been a useful member of Society) to drag out a miserable existence associated with the vilest and most degrading of society.'

She asked that mercy be shown and that her husband be allowed:

> 'after such punishment in this country as your Lordship in your human mercy may please to award, to return to his native place where petitioner (who has not seen him for four years) and her now fatherless offspring will not [illegible] to implore the Divine Blessing [upon the Recorder].

Neil Thompson petitioned twice. In a letter, undated but likely to be around late August or early September 1837 and sent from his cell in Newgate, Thompson laid out his reasons; not only did the judge sum up in Thompson's favour but 'the jury deliberated nearly half an hour'. They gave their verdict but recommended mercy understanding Thompson was not in a position to produce witnesses, 'but which verdict (even so qualified) seemed to astonish the audience in court'. Thompson maintained his innocence, claiming he was a 'victim of a cruel conspiracy' which he asked the Home Secretary to investigate. He had continued in the capacity of ship's mate on the *Heroine* for eleven months after the alleged offence and it was only after he had had a personal disagreement with Captain Murray that a charge was brought against him. With no trial, nor inquiries, taking place at Sierra Leone, Thompson was denied the opportunity to produce 'the only persons on board the ship at the Time besides the prosecutor and the said two witnesses'. Sent home in irons, Thompson considered he had only been acting to protect his employer's property. This was his first offence.

To add weight to his argument the charge was a conspiracy, Thompson gave details of independent attendees at the Old Bailey: J Hodgson, a solicitor from Wapping, London; a stranger to Thompson but 'who was casually present'; and Henry Buckland of Great Hermitage Street, Wapping. The men had observed the reactions of those speaking against the prisoner as they left the court, reporting they 'exulted at the verdict', with Mustard saying to Gillon, '"It's all right. We have done for the B–g–r"'. Thompson continued, 'And the other witness reproached the Prosecutor with "not having sworn hard enough" ...' and the people standing by 'exclaimed "shame!"'

From boyhood, Thompson had lead a sea-faring life. He had been chief mate on many ships and been well-regarded by his employers. In Scotland, he had an aged, widowed mother, and a wife and two children all dependent upon his support, without which they would be destitute. His conviction

had barred him from the reclaiming his wages but, he told the Home
Secretary, if the Crown informed the brig owners it 'waives the forfeiture
of the money due from them to the prisoner' he would be able to supply
his dependants with essential provisions. The brig was owned by Lawrie
and Hamilton Merchants, Cheapside, London. Thompson's petition was
undersigned by twenty-two supporters living in the area of Wapping, who
confirmed Thompson was a:

> 'steady and noble mariner – zealous for the interests of his
> Employers and we never heard anything to his disadvantage till
> the present charge which we have reason to believe originated in
> malice.'

The signatories include pilots, boat-builders, a ship's agent, and a draper.
This petition was sent to the Home Secretary via Robert Wallace, MP for
Greenock.

Thompson also wrote to Queen Victoria and described the incident at
the centre of his conviction. The *Heroine* was off Grand Batto and had
lost an anchor in the previous day's gale. Having only one anchor left,
the vessel needed to be watched and Thompson was left in charge whilst
Captain Murray was on shore. Tired from the exertions of the previous day,
Thompson had set the watches, given orders to Alexander Mustard on first
watch to alert him if necessary, and 'retired to his hammock about 9 o'clock'.
But around midnight, Thompson was roused by a noise and soon after he
was told by 'a Black woman and the Boy (the only persons on board but the
crew) … that the sailors were taking the liquor out of the cask.' Thompson
got up straightaway and found:

> 'the sails hanging lose to the yard and Henry Kemp the
> Prosecutor and Decampt another seaman coming abaft and on
> looking over the ship's side she appeared to him to be driving
> from her Anchor.'

Alarmed, Thompson thought the crew 'meditated some mischief' but when
he ordered them to tell him who had untied the sails, two sailors tried to grab
him from the Quarter Deck. Rushing to the Round House, he 'brought out
the Captain's Fowling piece to deter the men from violence'. The resulting
scuffle left Kemp suffering from a violent blow on the head and Thompson
severely beaten although he declared the stock of the gun was broken as a

result of it hitting the Round House. Thompson restored order and kept watch the rest of the night himself:

> 'the seamen being drunk and Lawson who had the second watch
> was lying speechless from intoxication on the Forecastle floor.'

Early the next day, Thompson sent a letter to the Captain, by canoe, and the Captain returned around 11 o'clock. Investigating, they discovered almost six gallons of grog was missing from the ship's stores, and a bottle of Gin and about four pounds of ham had been stored away in the Forecastle. Once events had been recorded in the ship's log, the Captain and Thompson debated for some time whether the crew should be prosecuted for Mutiny but by the time the brig arrived at Sierra Leone, the Captain prevailed on Thompson 'to pass it over and pardon them which he did.' According to the Judge's report in the Home Office correspondence, the brig had been carrying cloths, boards and guns with a value in excess of £6000.

Thompson continued as mate but by April the men provoked a quarrel between Thompson and the Captain by telling 'false stories' and this resulted in the charge against him. With the log book withheld from him and Captain Murray in Africa, he had nothing to counter the claims of his prosecutor.

On 7 September 1837, John William Hamilton, co-owner of the *Heroine*, wrote to the Home Secretary from Cheapside, regarding Thompson's case:

> 'From the best information I am able to obtain, it appears to me that
> he committed the crime under some strong mental delusion and
> not from any premediated intentions to injure the men, or to obtain
> possession of their property.'

Hamilton suggested a combination of alcohol and 'the extreme heat of the climate' had resulted in Thompson committing the offence and requested his sentence be mitigated 'so far as may appear consistent with the punishment due to his crime.'

Robert Wallace MP continued to support Thompson's case as did W.H. Campbell, MP for Argyllshire, to whom Thompson's mother, Mary Turner, turned to for help. Mary Turner, widow of John MacTavish (or Thomson) wrote from Lochgilphead, Argyllshire, on 27 September 1837. Her son had tried to suppress a mutiny, she claimed, and was acting in self-defence. Her letter was undersigned by six supporters who confirm Neil Thompson's 'humane and civil disposition.' This was forwarded, by W.H. Campbell who, in his covering letter, asked the Honourable Charles Gore to put the petition in front of Lord John Russell, 'and tell him I really wish he could grant the prayer of the petition.'

A petition was also sent from twelve supporters 'on behalf of a well-deserving well-behaved and industrious woman', Jane Thompson. The signatories included Robert Wallace MP, a bailie (the Scottish equivalent of a magistrate in England), a surgeon, three ministers and two magistrates. They ask that Thompson should be allowed to stay in this country, otherwise 'a wife will lose a beloved husband and a family an affectionate Parent'. It was answered on 14 December 1837. Neil Thompson had embarked for Van Diemen's Land on the *Moffat*, on 27 October 1837.

The Judge, Mr Justice Williams, wrote to the Home Secretary on 31 October 1837 having consulted his own notes from the trial. He stated that the only question the Jury had to answer was whether or not they believed the prosecution evidence; if they did, it would be to believe 'great and wholly unprovoked violence'. Although he had no written reminder:

> 'I have no doubt that I did remark (for the consideration of the Jury) upon the perfect absence of all cause for the outrage the Prosecutor having admitted in answer to questions put by myself, that there never had been a particle of difference between himself and the prisoner up to the moment of the transaction.'

The jury were aware Thompson had continued as mate even though the captain was immediately abreast of the incident and all its details; they also knew of 'the defenceless state of the prisoner as to witnesses...' The Judge pointed out that Thompson's written character references were from local people and had they been called a different result might have ensued. It had been suggested 'that liquor and heat had disordered the prisoner's intellect.'

Supporting mitigation, the judge added, 'nothing could be more grateful to my feelings than that good reasons may be discovered for any quantity of mitigation in the sentence.' This letter is annotated, by the Home Secretary 'Transportation for life, in such a case, seems exceedingly severe. Commute to ten years.' This comment is undated but a separate annotation notes, 'Commute to 10 years transportation 8 December 1837'.

On 10 May 1841, Robert Wallace MP wrote to Lord John Russell, now Secretary of State for War and the Colonies, reminding him of Thompson's case and asking for a free pardon if Thompson's conduct in Van Diemen's Land merited it. He reiterated the respectability of the earlier supporting petitioners and added that Thompson's family were 'in abject misery in consequence of his absence.' The War and Colonial Office annotation notes, 'The usual course', and Wallace's letter was sent on to Phillipps for the Home Secretary's consideration. On 1 June 1841, it seems a letter was sent back to the War and Colonial Office, the annotation being 'If conduct good in colony Free Pardon.'

Enquiries were made of the Lieutenant-Governor of Van Diemen's Land and in April 1842 it was reported Thompson's behaviour did not justify a free pardon straightaway but if his behaviour proved him deserving of mercy in the meantime, he would receive a Free Pardon 'on the next anniversary of the Queen's birthday...'

Very different circumstances gave rise to the conviction of **Gregorio Guinea**, who was charged with stabbing a person with intent to murder and was tried at the Old Bailey, November Sessions, 1833. Found guilty, he was sentenced to death.

Gregorio Guinea, a Spaniard from Burgos, arrived in England on 26 January 1833. His Home Office petition case notes he was 46 years old, (as also appears in the account of his trial at the Old Bailey[3]), but it is possible that he was over ten years older. Ship's surgeon's records of the following year state he is sixty. In his communications with the Home Office, Guinea gave his profession as a naval officer who had been expelled from Spain.

Having been proscribed in his native country, Guinea had made his way to England but, unable to speak or understand English, he had fallen on hard times. He had left the French depot of Poitiers with his friend Manuel Mariluz (or Marcilan), and in England Mariluz had successfully applied to the Government fund which was designed to help refugees. But whilst Mariluz had received £15, Guinea's application was rejected. The fund was supervised by Domingo Maria Ruiz de la Vega, of Symon's Wharf, Tooley Street, Southwark, and in one of Guinea's four petitions to the Home Office, written with the help of supporters, he explained how he had come to believe his rejection was due to the 'prejudiced reports of two persons named Escober and La Vega'.

Guinea had hoped to return to Spain but without funds he was, he explained, 'doomed to wander about here in a state of great privation and distress'. He had tried several times to have his name added to the list for relief provided by 'this Benevolent and Generous Government' but whether true or imagined, de la Vega stood in his way. In the intervening months, Guinea twice challenged de la Vega to a duel, then on 11 October 1833, having taken 'some ardent spirits' with other Spaniards, he attacked de la Vega with a knife. Guinea described the incident as taking place in 'one of the greatest public thoroughfares in London' and de la Vega prosecuted. Guinea was indicted and brought for trial in front of Mr Justice Littledale at the Old Bailey, where he was charged on five counts related to maliciously assaulting Domingo Maria Ruiz de la Vega with a knife, stabbing and wounding with intent to kill, maim, disable and grievous bodily harm him.

The Times newspaper carried a report in 17 October 1833 in the section headed 'Police', sub-headed 'Mansion House', which tells of Guinea (here 'Guinas') being brought before the Lord Mayor on 16 October. They describe Guinea as a 'wretched, sallow-looking object' and de la Vega as a Spanish refugee who came to England many years ago and who was held in high regard by those who had been appointed to administer the relief funds for refugees in financial need.

According to the report, witnesses were brought forward to confirm the attack. Mr Estworthy, an employee at one of the Thames Street wharfs, had been passing near London Bridge at around half-past two the previous Friday and saw Guinea make a sudden dash towards his victim and hit him across the legs with 'a sharp instrument'. Despite Estworthy's attempts to intervene and stop the attack, Guinea struck de la Vega again, this time around the head. de la Vega called 'murder' but received another strike around the head from which blood gushed as he attempted to flee. Estworthy described Guinea as being 'quite infuriate' and although he tried to run off, he was apprehended.

E. Gaskyll, an employee of the *Sun* said he saw the bloodied de la Vega after Guinea had run at him. Benjamin Hager was standing at the top of Cannon Street and witnessed two people scuffling and, like Estworthy, saw Guinea strike his victim. Hager too had tried to intervene. Witness Mr Meazette attempted to prevent the prisoner escaping and, despite Guinea's attempts to deter him by thrusting his knife in his direction, Meazette managed to knock the knife from the attacker. Guinea was then apprehended by a police officer and other witnesses. The knife was shown in court and the report described it as seeming to be a very sharp and well-used gardening knife.

Although the newspaper suggested that the prisoner was not believed when he said he could not understand English, at his trial, Guinea spoke through an interpreter. He pleaded guilty three times despite the judge advising him to retract it, and Guinea was sentenced to death.

Guinea was distraught; he had not expected so severe a sentence. In his petitions, he claimed his crime in Spain would have carried only 12–18 months imprisonment. de la Vega petitioned on Guinea's behalf, as did George R. Devereux, a lieutenant in the Royal Marines. In addition to language problems and his ignorance of the law, Guinea claimed that alcohol had influenced him; he had had been suffering hardship, his health was failing (he stated he had two hernias) and his wife and child in Spain were worried about him. The crime was not pre-meditated, he was contrite and the victim was not mortally wounded.

His case was considered at King in Council 5 February 1834 and after further deliberation, Guinea's sentence was commuted to one year's imprisonment with three months solitary and then transportation for life.

It seems that from Newgate prison, Guinea was sent straight to the *York* hulk ship at Portsmouth but it is possible that he served time at the Bridewell. He embarked on the *Mangles* for Van Diemen's Land in April 1835, just after Devereux had sent his petition.

Gregorio Guinea is mentioned in the ship's surgeon's journal. Here his age is given as sixty and he was put on the sick list on 20 July 1835, 'at sea' and 'discharged to duty' on 24 July. The reason given is 'vulnus' (a wound). The entry continues:

'Struck on the face by a [bullet of round] thrown by an unknown hand while eating dinner quietly on deck, the integuments covering the chin were divided and he was laid prostrate for a minute or two, there was some bleeding which stopped when the edges of the wound were brought together.'

Records in the Tasmanian Archives give further details. Guinea is described here as 5ft 6in tall, with grey hair, grey eyes, a high, 'wrinkled' forehead, a brown complexion and aged forty-three. He had not seen his wife for three years and had relatives in Madrid. His occupation is listed as 'Captain Spanish Service', ('soldier' is crossed out). He was unable to speak English, his hulk report was 'very good', his surgeon's report stated 'quiet' but he had been convicted before for a similar offence. Two incidents of absconding in 1836 and 1837 would led to punishments of hard labour. He died on 27 January 1839.

On 1 January 1824, at the end of his tether and fuelled by jealousy stoked by suspected infidelity, **William Henry Reynolds** strode to the house of the man he believed was his wife's lover and shot him. Twice. His victim, General Napier Christie (or Christian) Burton, survived the attack and prosecuted. Reynolds, who considered himself to be the wronged man, was now to face the death penalty.

William Reynolds was a 40-year-old carpenter, born in Maidstone, Kent, described in the Newgate Register of Prisoners as 5ft 9in, of 'stoutish' build, with brown hair, grey eyes and a 'sallow' complexion. On 14 January 1824, at Justice Hall, Old Bailey, he was charged on three counts relating to General Burton: shooting with intent to murder; shooting with intent to disable; shooting with intent to do his victim grievous bodily harm. Reynolds was found guilty but the jury strongly recommended mercy due to his previous good character. He was sentenced to death and sent back to Newgate prison.

Petitions from Reynolds, his supporters, and associated Home Office documentation, provide details of Reynold's life and the circumstances which led to his crime. At the time of his attack on General Burton, Reynolds had been married to Elizabeth Matilda Meadley for six years, their wedding appearing to have taken place on 10 June 1818, at Saint Mary's church in Newington, London.[4] The couple had three children, all under the age of four and lived at 2, Little Peter Street, Sun Street, Bishopsgate, London.

From his cell in Newgate whilst under sentence of death, Reynolds petitioned the King three times. He explained how he had 'now living three children, whom he hath most tenderly and affectionately soucored and supported with all the humanity as a parent.' But his wife 'whom he most dearly loved' had been persuaded, by someone, to leave the family on three occasions, each absence lasting between ten days and a fortnight. Distressed, Reynolds made enquiries and discovered Elizabeth had made frequent visits to General Burton. On 1 January 1824, after Elizabeth had been away from her husband for nine days, Reynolds went to General Burton's house and found his wife in the parlour, wearing unfamiliar dress and drinking wine with the General. 'Enraged with jealousy and revenge' towards the man Reynolds believed had been keeping Elizabeth from her family, Reynolds shot him. Now, he felt 'the utmost sorrow and shudders with horror when he reflects on the dreadful deed...' Full of contrition, and gratitude for the General's survival, he requested his own life be spared for the sake of his innocent children.

Reynolds asked the King to consider:

'... those peculiar circumstances of his case, which although stated in the depositions of his Witnesses, were passed over in silence upon his trial.'

These, he hoped, would show the reasons why he had been so jealous of General Burton, 'illfounded as it may have been...' and hoped his failure to kill the General was evidence of a mind in disarray. The first petition had been undersigned by 211 local people and all 12 Jury members; the second was undersigned by 82 people from the parish of Saint Botolph's, Bishopsgate; the third petition, by 43 supporters.

With Reynolds still facing execution, Elizabeth petitioned the King, claiming that her husband's suspicions were unfounded but his worries had been played upon by people who were not sympathetic to her, 'so that he scarcely knew what he did.' Her letter was undersigned by thirty-three supporters. William Reynold's case was considered by the King in Council, 19 March 1824, and it is likely that it was here that Reynolds' sentence was commuted to transportation for life.

At Reynolds' trial[5], the court heard that General Burton had first become acquainted with Elizabeth's father, George Meadley, when both men were in the 6th Battalion of 60th Regiment of Foot. According to the General's evidence, and Elizabeth's petition, George Meadley had been promoted to ensign in 1806 on General Burton's recommendation. However, Meadley was assassinated in Jamaica and General Burton had procured pensions for both Elizabeth and her mother, Sarah. Elizabeth's amounted to £8 a year. The general, who gave his status as 'unmarried' had not seen Elizabeth for many years until they met again around December 1822.

According to a later petition from Reynolds, Elizabeth had become re-acquainted with General Burton in early 1823. She applied to him for the 'Register of her Baptism' as he was her godfather 'by Proxy'. The general was living in Paddington, London, and with their acquaintance re-established, he invited Elizabeth to renew her visits. Reynolds considered the general 'a great and valued Friend' with his offers of support and presents of game and fruit.

In the late autumn of 1823, Elizabeth gave birth but the child did not survive and around ten days after her confinement, General Burton visited Elizabeth. But when the general declined to leave his carriage, Elizabeth got out of bed and went to the general instead. Not long after the general's visit, Elizabeth began to complain of feeling unwell, and Reynolds agreed that she should go to her relations in Alvechurch, Worcestershire. Reynolds booked the coach and paid the fare for her and one of their children, aged two, whilst Elizabeth informed the general of her plans. However, when Reynolds checked upon his wife's safe arrival in Alvechurch, the coach guard told him she had only travelled around six miles, having got off at the first stage.

Making further investigations, Reynolds discovered his wife and their child, 'by various Conveyances, evidently for the purpose of aluding pursuit and detection' had come back to London and gone to Hatton Garden. Within two days, he received a letter from her, giving no indication of her precise whereabouts, but saying she was only four miles 'out of Town' and 'much better in health than when she left her House and would not return for some time'. This letter is included in the Home Office case file, and in it Elizabeth acknowledged her husband will be surprised to read from whence the letter comes but laid down the reasons for it:

> 'I was so very ill on monday morning that I could not get any farther than about a mile from Highgate where I got some breakfast and returned towards London by the holoway road intending to come home but as I found I could not make myself happy and you were agreeable for me to stay away a little while and as it will be no more expence or trouble to you than if I had gone on to the country I intend to remain here till the latter end of next week or the beginning of the week after when you may expect to see me I hope better than I am at present.'

After informing him the baby was well, hoped for the same for everyone at home and that Reynold's leg was better, she continued 'and when I come back I will make you as happy as I can...' She urged him not to worry about her: she didn't need anything and had 'found benefit from the air already'. After signing herself 'your affectionate wife Elizabeth Reynolds', as if an afterthought, Elizabeth dissuaded Reynolds from contacting the general until after she'd returned home:

> 'as he will think we are always troubling him and you I hope will not be angry with me as it was your own wish that I [illegible] be away from you if I could not be more happy than I was...'

She promised she would tell Reynolds, on her return, what had troubled her and that he didn't need to tell everybody where she was. She ended, 'God Bless you. E.R.'

Reynolds disregarded Elizabeth's suggestion and 'labouring under a state of mind more easily imagined than described' he visited the general to see if he knew of Elizabeth's location. General Burton 'appeared much agitated, and expressed great surprise at her conduct...' He told Reynolds he didn't know where Elizabeth was but thought she would write to him when she needed anything. With Reynold's suspicions growing, he visited the general two or three times more times, noticing that the general seemed increasingly confused to the extent that at times he was 'scarcely capable of articulating answers' to the questions Reynolds asked:

> '... and repeatedly wished, that, whenever the Servant entered the Room, your Memorialist would talk about the Moon or Stars, or anything other than the direct question until he was gone...'

Throughout these conversations, the General maintained that he was ignorant of Elizabeth's whereabouts, but when he admitted he had seen her, Reynolds asked him if he had given Elizabeth money.

> 'After a silence of some minutes and great agitation [the General told Reynolds] he had given her a Pound to keep her from Prostitution until he could reconcile her and your Memorialist together again as he was sure there must have been some cause for her leaving your Memorialist.'

More than twenty days later, Elizabeth returned home, her luggage being transported by the Highgate Stage. When pressed, Elizabeth told her husband only that she had:

> 'been very comfortable and wanted for nothing, and that she knew your Memorialist would take care of the Children.'

She remained at home for three weeks and then left without hint or warning. Reynolds was at a loss what to do, feeling sure it wasn't anything he had done that had caused her to leave. Once again, he asked the general if he knew where Elizabeth was staying; once again, the general expressed ignorance and confusion.

At the trial at the Old Bailey, General Burton said Elizabeth visited him on 26 December 1823 around 11.00 o'clock in the morning and he wrote to Reynolds, who upon receiving the letter, went to the general's house in New Street, Dorset Square. The general expressed surprise that the letter had reached Reynolds so quickly – Reynolds was at the door at 5 o'clock that afternoon. When Reynolds asked if his wife was going to return to him, the general had told him he didn't know and that Elizabeth appeared scared. He did not see her again, he said, until 1 January 1824.

Reynolds feared the general was only acting as his friend in order to seduce Elizabeth and after her 'second flight' he felt sure of it. His feelings reached 'a pitch of frenzy' so much so that, despairing, he bought two pistols. He admitted his intention was to kill the general, 'the Author of his wrongs' – and then himself.

At the trial the general described the events of Thursday, 1 January 1824, telling how Reynolds had arrived at his house in late afternoon. Elizabeth was already there and the general offered Reynolds wine and was handing him the glass when Reynolds fired his first shot. Feeling nothing himself, the general feared Elizabeth had been the intended target. He had tried to calm Reynolds down but when he got closer, Reynolds fired a second shot, this time at the general's right side. He now realised that he was the intended victim and knew he had been wounded.

An exchange between the two men ensued, in which Reynolds confirmed he had bought the balls two days previously in Norton Folgate, a street running between Shoreditch and Bishopsgate. He told the general he had loaded the pistols himself and had left his victim in no doubt as to his purpose and pleasure at shooting him. The commotion had alerted Burton's servants, the watchman was called and the general sent for surgeon, James Lock. When asked in front of witnesses, Reynolds repeated that his intention was to shoot the general. In fact, one ball had missed and the other had only grazed the general's side. Lock told the court if the bullet been a little higher, it would have gone into his lungs and killed him.

According to the general, Reynolds seemed devastated when the balls were found; both men had thought the balls had penetrated and Reynolds knew he would be punished for his actions. Reynolds produced a soiled and ripped letter and threw it on the table and Elizabeth grabbed it. Reynolds later implied that the general had written it but Elizabeth gave the general the letter who passed it to James Lock. When Lock read out the letter in court, it was anonymous but addressed to Reynolds and dated 21 December 1823. It suggested his wife would not have left him without provocation and indirectly accused him of being a drunken gambler who didn't care about his family. Reynolds accused the general of betraying his trust but the general insisted that Reynolds was mistaken.

In his later petition, Reynolds gave his version of the events of 1 January 1824, writing that when he reached the General's house he found Elizabeth 'dressed in the gayest and most costly style, taking wine with him, and appearances were as if they'd just dined'. He continued, 'Confusion and agitation seized all…' because Reynolds' visit had not been expected and he had allowed the general's servant no time to alert his master to the surprise visitor. The general recovered himself and offered Reynolds wine, but feeling his worst suspicions had been confirmed and 'goaded on by the taunts of his wife' Reynolds fired two shots at him. Luckily, he was unharmed and Reynolds gave himself up without a struggle, thankful that he had not killed anyone.

Reynolds made no defence at his trial, but nine character witnesses spoke in his favour, as being even-tempered and mild.

William Reynolds was not the only one with suspicions about the true nature of the relationship between Elizabeth and the general and he had many sympathisers. On 29 January 1824, just over two weeks after the trial, Archdeacon Blomfield, Rector of St Botolph's, Bishopsgate, had written requesting an interview with the Home Secretary, Robert Peel. The following day, he wrote again to the Home Secretary regarding Reynolds' case, transmitting eleven witness depositions taken by the defence attorney. He pointed out that they were not referred to in court, due to 'the shameful negligence of the Attorney who seems not to have retained Counsel till a very few minutes before the trial came on.' The witnesses who had given depositions were only called to give character references. As a result of this omission, Archdeacon Blomfield wrote, the jury had made their decision 'under the impression' that Reynolds' jealously was unfounded:

'General Burton having disclaimed all connexion with the woman, although he admitted that she was found in his house, sitting with him after dinner and drinking wine.'

The Archdeacon drew particular attention to the witness statements of Sayers, Goddin and Witt and suggested that the jury's verdict might have been different had they been given those facts; 'as it was they were thirty five minutes in deliberation'. The depositions throw more light on the relationship between Reynolds and Elizabeth and their lives and circumstances before they met, as well as the relationship between Elizabeth and General Burton. Also attached to the list of those depositions, in a hand without signature, is an explanatory note on the character and thus integrity, of the witnesses, for instance, Mr Jones of 7, Brook Street, New Road, Fitzroy Square:

'Mr Jones keeps a small cabinet makers shop has been there some time and bears a good character';

Elizabeth Goddin of 29, Hatton Wall:

> '... goes out Nursing and bears an excellent character in the Neighbourhood.'

It is noted that Mr Blades, living at 44, Holland Street, Blackfriars Road:

> '... was employed at the Sessions House, and I believe you know more of him than I can inform you.'

Charles Sayers had been lodging with the Reynolds', in Little Peter Street, for one and three quarter years at the time he gave his statement in January 1824. When he was first there, Reynolds and Elizabeth had 'lived very comfortably together' but about four months ago they had an argument. The cause of their disagreement was the amount of attention Elizabeth was paying to another of their lodgers, a young man called Lambert, and that attention was more than she was giving her husband. But Sayers confirmed Reynolds 'was always very fond of his wife' and it was about a month after their argument that, with Reynolds' consent, she went to the country for health reasons. According to Sayers he heard Reynolds say that Elizabeth had gone on the Worcester coach but came back:

> '... by another coach, to some place near Hyde Park Corner, whence she took a porter to carry her box for about a mile, when she took a Hackney coach in to Holborn.'

Reynolds couldn't trace her movements after that and she did not return for seven days. When Elizabeth came home she had 'refused to say where she'd been; but professed great attachment to Lambert.'

Sayers confirmed that General Burton had visited the Reynolds' home about a fortnight later:

> 'where he was received by Reynolds and his wife, Reynolds having formerly spoken of General Burton as a kind friend to him and his wife.'

Approximately three weeks afterwards, Sayers's own wife told him Elizabeth Reynolds had remarked to her that:

> 'she (Mrs Reynolds) would not know what to say to General Burton when he came, for that she had told General Burton, when at his

house, that she was not in the family way whereas in fact she was
so; and Deponent's wife further told him that General Burton had
just been there and that Mrs Reynolds went out and remained with
him about twenty minutes in a hackney coach, not having been put
to bed at that time more than ten days.'

Reynolds had worried continually that General Burton was taking Elizabeth
away from him, 'and appeared greatly distressed, crying like a child, saying
that he should never be happy again.' That the general had sent many presents was confirmed by Sayers 'and that she was considered by the neighbours not to be true to her husband.'

Mrs Sayers stated Elizabeth had seemed happy with Reynolds until she
met General Burton, approximately 18 months before, but since Elizabeth's
'15 or 20' meetings with him, her affection towards her husband and family
had decreased. On various occasions, when Elizabeth had returned home
'she had expressed her dissatisfaction with various articles & compelled her
husband to purchase new furniture'. Mrs Sayers confirmed the General had
given presents, and had visited twice; one time he did not leave his coach
and the other the servant went in, but Elizabeth had gone to his hackney
coach where she sat with him for half an hour.

Elizabeth Goddin had known Elizabeth since before she had married
Reynolds and the latter had told Goddin that the General had visited often in
the last eighteen months: 'I think she told me of about 10 times'. The reason
she gave Goddin was that the General was a very good friend who knew her
father and mother and that, 'she could command anything she liked & was
always a welcome visitor.' When Goddin saw Elizabeth's scent box, Elizabeth
told her the general had given it to her; she had fainted, and on coming round
on his sofa found the general had sent his servant for scent which he then told
her to keep. Goddin also recounted how Elizabeth had told her:

> '... shortly after one of her visits last summer that the General had
> asked her if she was completely comfortable with her husband.'

If she wasn't, the general would try and get her a separation for her 'on
account of her not being of age on her marriage' and he had 'offered her
asylum at his country house which she said she thought she should accept.'
When Goddin asked Elizabeth about this matter 'about a week later',
Elizabeth thought now she would go Worcester, and believed the general
would give her £5 for 'her expenses'.

Through Goddin's statement comes the information that Reynolds had been a widower before he married Elizabeth. Goddin knew William Reynolds 'when his first wife was living, & he always appeared very affectionate and kind to both her and the latter'. She remarked that after Elizabeth had left then returned the second time, Reynolds had employed a woman to look after the family and Elizabeth and he then 'appeared quite comfortable and reconciled.'

The churchwardens at St Botolph's, Bishopsgate, with Mr White, the defence attorney, had interviewed General Burton on 11 February 1824, this information being sent to the Home Office. According to the general, he was aware Elizabeth 'was married to two husbands' since the beginning of their re-acquaintance and both husbands were alive. She was also receiving a pension but to access it 'she had to swear, four times every year, she was a single woman'. The general admitted to the churchwardens that he had met Elizabeth frequently but claimed he had become involved in her affairs and 'interfered to prevent dispute between her and her husband'. He claimed that he had told Elizabeth to go home once, and wrote to Reynolds to say she had visited him, but then when Reynolds turned up at his house 'immediately', he had denied knowledge of her whereabouts. Elizabeth had stayed near Highgate instead of going to Worcestershire relatives. The churchwardens' note continues:

> 'It appears General Burton has a Villa at Highgate to which Mrs Reynolds had frequent invitations.'

William Cavillier was perhaps one of those to whom Elizabeth referred when she wrote of people unsympathetic to her in her petition to the King. His relationship to Elizabeth is not indicated but Cavillier made no secret of his feelings for her in a letter sent from Whitby on 12 January 1824. The vitriolic comments suggest great familiarity; he is replying to a letter from Reynolds' mother. After receiving 'your distressing letter' Cavillier 'immediately wrote to the General Burton, Petitioning him for your worthy son in the name of my Wife…' He calls Elizabeth 'the Devil Incarnate' and a 'wretch' who:

> 'has been a Blot upon the Creation of the Almighty's Works ever since she was ten years of age and Many's the unhappy hours we have had, Night and Day, through her. Her disposition is such that she delights in making every one Miserable that she has to do with.'

Imprisoned in Newgate, William Reynolds suffered mental and physical ill-health. In May 1826, the surgeon to the gaol, W. Box, stated in a certificate that although Reynolds' health had improved since the winter, 'there is every reason to believe if his imprisonment is prolonged it will prove fatal to him as he is evidently consumptive.' On 27 July 1826, Blomfield, now Bishop of Chester, contacted Henry Hobhouse, Under-Secretary of State at the Home Office. Reynolds had written to one of Bishop Chester's parishioners and Chester was concerned that Reynolds was ill in the infirmary at Newgate 'without a chance of being restored to health, without a change of air'. He added:

> '[Reynold's case is] not one which admitted of his liberation. If this were intimated to him from authority, his friends would be spared the pain of making repeated applications through me without any satisfactory result.'

Less than three weeks later, Reynolds was moved from Newgate. On 15 August, he was sent to the *Dolphin* hulk at Chatham, and then to the hospital ship *Canada* also anchored there. In June the following year, he wrote to the Home Secretary, William Sturges Bourne, from the *Canada*, outlining his case in more detail, including the background to events, and asking for a pardon. He added that he had 'received the greatest consolation from religious instruction which has always been afforded to him as well as every other human attention possible'. His letter was transmitted by A.W. Robarts, on 2 July 1827, via Spencer Percival in the Home Office. But Reynolds' request was unsuccessful; the Home Office annotation states 'Refused', ten days later.

In April 1828, Reynolds was one of four prisoners, (three from the *Dolphin* hulk, and one from the *Canada*), to be recommended to John H. Capper, the superintendent of prison hulks, for mitigation of their sentence. They had been selected by Captain George Lloyd as 'fit objects' and the occasion was 'on the anniversary of his Majesty's birthday'. Reynolds, number 1942 in the ship's register, is noted as having served four years, three months and nine days of his sentence. The gaoler's report states he is:

> 'A very good carpenter in which capacity he has been employed here, but owing to the delicate state of his Health it is considered desirable he should be removed from this Gaol.'

One of the four prisoners, John Winkley, did not have his sentence reduced but Reynolds had better luck. The annotation suggests the outcome was a remission in his sentence from transportation for life to transportation for fourteen years on 28 April 1828.

Chapter 9

Words from New South Wales and Van Diemen's Land

1 00,000 convicts, including 13,000 women, were transported from Britain to Australian penal colonies between 1788 and 1836. By the time transportation ended, the total would exceed 160,000, peaking in the 1820s and 1830s and declining sharply from the middle of the century.

Although convicts had been arriving in Van Diemen's Land since 1803, it was the 1820s, 1830s and first half of 1840s which saw the greatest numbers arrive there, as transportation to alternative Australian penal colonies ceased. 10,338 convicts arrived in Van Dieman's Land between 1 January 1831-31 December 1835, and 9,142 between 1 January 1836-31 December 1840.

During the 1820s and 1830s, most convict employment was as assignment to individual employers or the establishment and the number of those enjoying a level of freedom, within boundaries, significantly increased. Good conduct by the prisoner could lead to a reduction in sentence and eventual liberty through a series of stages; a licence and pardons. The licence or ticket of leave was initially a flexibly applied form of reward for the prisoner and a way to save Government money, but rules for eligibility were established by Sir Thomas Brisbane, the governor of New South Wales from 1821 to 1825. These rules for a person receiving a life sentence are clearly explained in a letter between a convict's mother and his employer.

18-year-old **Charles Rich** was a drover from Romford, Essex. He stood trial at the Old Bailey, in October 1836, accused of stealing sheep belonging to James Meakins. Found guilty, Rich was sentenced to transportation for life. He had been recommended for mercy by the jury on account of his previous good behaviour and petitions were sent to the Home Office begging a mitigation of sentence but these were unsuccessful and marked 'Nil'.

Rich was first sent to the *York* hulk, then transported to New South Wales on the *Mangles*, arriving in 1837. He was assigned as a servant to work on the estate of William Dumaresq at St Aubins, Scone. Rich's mother, Elizabeth, was desperate for news of her son and she wrote to Dumaresq in July 1839, asking about her son's health and well-being.

William Dumaresq's reply of 19 March 1840 demonstrates a respect and concern for those working for him. After acknowledging receipt of Mrs Rich's letter, Dumaresq assures her, not only that her son is aware of his mother's love, but that his future is good if he behaves himself well, writing:

'He has seen the letter you have sent me and I cannot but hope that your anxiety and the warm affection you evince for him, will meet with a proper return, and that his conduct here will be such that he will merit and receive, all the indulgence which the laws of the country allow – of personal comfort, if he's steady and attentive, he has a much as he would probably have as a labouring man in any country.'

Dumaresq shows confidence in his 'assigned servant':

'When he first came I had reason to fear he was disposed to be a little irregular, and would give some trouble. I hope better of him now and that he is convinced that it is by being steady and useful that his own ends will be best obtained.'

Elizabeth Rich's original letter is not with her son's Home Office petition case, but she had concerns regarding his future inheritance, as evidenced by Dumaresq's reply and his clear explanation of the legal position of someone such as Rich:

'As regards the points you mention of his inheriting a portion of your property – in his present condition he is ineligible, and it must be many years before he can be so to inherit property in England. He is sentenced to this country for <u>Life</u>. An Act of Parliament provides that he must serve here 8 years before he can obtain the indulgence of a <u>Ticket of Leave</u>, which does not, under the present law, allow him to hold property, but merely to employ himself in a fixed district, and under certain Regulations exclusively for his own advantage, that is, he employs himself with whom and in what manner he likes, being under no restraint in his agreements for service in this condition he must remain 6 years <u>blameless</u> before he will become eligible for what is termed a <u>Conditional Pardon</u>, with this he is Free in every respect to possess property etc. <u>in this</u>

<u>country</u>, but he cannot leave it – if in this state he conducts himself well, and can show by his good moral behaviour and his industry that he might be trusted to go to his Native Country again, under a proper Representation he may obtain an <u>Absolute Pardon</u> which restores him to all his Civil Rights in England or elsewhere, when of course he can receive and inherit property – any property I imagine you might wish to devise him, could be done so in <u>trust</u> to him on his obtaining his absolute Freedom or to his heirs … His case must be urged very strongly with great interest, in England to obtain him any remission beyond what I have pointed out – of this you must be the best judge.'

Having given Elizabeth Rich his advice, and perhaps a glimmer of hope that she might see her son again, Dumaresq's next words might contain a note of reality for his chances or that even then, for a young man, opportunities may eventually seem brighter in New South Wales:

'I can only say that if he conducts himself well he may be very happy and establish himself well in the Country, as I dare say he will have told you. The best thing I can tell you at present is, that I do not hear of any complaints of him from my overseer.'

Dumaresq closes the letter respecting Elizabeth Rich's motherly anxiety for her son's spiritual as well as bodily welfare, by concluding:

'Hoping you may live to have the assurances that his moral and religious character is what you would desire it to be. I remain yours obediently Wm Dumaresq.'

According to New South Wales Archives, Rich obtained a ticket of leave in 1848 and a conditional pardon in August 1850, but does not appear to have acquired an absolute pardon which would have allowed him to return home and see his mother and family.

William Gibson was tried at the Old Bailey, December Sessions 1831, accused of housebreaking and stealing 'plate' above the value of £5. His victim and prosecutor was Gilbert Ainsley Young of Portland Place, London. Gibson was found guilty and sentenced to death. His case was considered at a Report in Council on 6 February 1832 and there his sentence was commuted to transportation for life.

Gibson petitioned the Home Secretary, Lord Melbourne, with his letter undersigned by fourteen supporters. Three petitions were sent by his father, J. Gibson, who also enclosed two letters from his son. William Gibson claimed he had been entrapped, was contrite and the prosecutor recommended mercy. In addition, his health was impaired by imprisonment and his family were distraught.

Gibson was sent from Newgate to Middlesex House of Correction and wrote to his father from '4 Ward North Side' on 9 February 1832. He understood six months in the House of Correction would form part of his punishment before being transported, but his health was suffering and harsh discipline would make it worse. He asked if this could be commuted but if that was not possible requests he be allowed 'some books which may be necessary to perfect my knowledge of my Business…'

Maria Gibson had been married to William less than a year when he received his sentence; the couple had married on 23 May 1831. He was now still only twenty and she a year older. However, in April 1832, he sailed on the *England* and arrived in Van Diemen's Land in July 1832. Maria Gibson wrote to Lord Melbourne.

On 29 April 1832, she thanked him for sparing her husband's life but said she had 'another favour to beg of your Lordship'; she wanted to follow Gibson abroad, declaring as an incentive for the Home Secretary's approval:

> 'I am thoroughly convinced that if we should be fortunate enough again to meet, I shall be a check to him in his future life [and help him regain his reputation and honour] I see Nothing in this Country before me but Poverty, and Distress. My friends and relations have all of them set their faces against me in consequence of the thoughtless conduct of my husband'.

She believed she would be unable to find herself employment because of the 'too severe shock' her character has received. The Home Secretary did not agree to her request, and her petition is marked 'Nil', 'She cannot join him'.

According to Tasmanian Archives, Gibson was 5ft 5½in tall 'without shoes', had a fair complexion, small head, brown hair, brown small whiskers, dark grey eyes and a low perpendicular forehead. His age is given as twenty-two.

William Gibson's father was a surveyor and William had been his clerk. On 3 September 1833 William Gibson wrote to 'My Dear Parents' from Hobart Town, Van Diemen's Land. He tells them that he received their letter of February in mid-August and thanks them for the £2 they sent him which he assures then 'came at a very reasonable time'. It seems this was not his first letter because he tells them he is in the same job, as clerk at the Board of Assignment. This, he acknowledges has been helped by his good luck on arrival 'to be placed under a very good master Viz James Thorneloe Esq' who has 'kindly offered' to confirm Gibson's good behaviour by a report at the end of the letter. Gibson continues:

'I have now been out of the Prisoner's Barracks about 7 months and hold a memorandum from the Governor (in consequence of my good conduct) to employ myself for my own advantage after Government hours which are from 9 till 3 which would be very advantageous to me was there anything to be done but business here at this time of the year (Depth of Winter) is quite at a stand still, but upon the whole I have no cause of complaint excepting being Banished from my Parents and Native Land.'

Gibson expresses his hope that he'll have a good future:

'If a Prisoner behaves well he is sure to be treated well, if on the other hand he once forgets himself in the slightest way he knows not when or where his misery may end.'

He assures his parents they can take comfort from the fact:

'I am going on very steady as I find that strictly adhering to the rules laid down is the best course to follow.'

Outlining his routine, Gibson tells his family:

'I am residing with a Brother Clerk in misfortune at [illegible] Argyle Street we each pay 2/0 per week for Lodging only then comes our washing which amounts to something more say 2/4 per week and then comes eating etc which at this season is very expensive. I arise every morning at about ¼ before 8 wash dress and breakfast and reach the office at 9 where I am engaged until 3. I then at am liberty to go where I please till 8 in the evening at which time the whole of the Prisoner Population (residing within the Rules) must be at their place of residence, so it continues every day till Sunday. I have then to go to Church with about 30 more poor Scribblers at ½ past 10 to answer names which done we proceed to Church till One o'clock afternoon 1/2 past 3 till 6. So much for a few comforts the Prisoners ever enjoy I am not able to give you much description of the miseries the Punishments are various Viz Score Flogging, Working in the Roads, Chain Gangs, the Hulk and lastly Penal Settlements are always in attendance should you transgress.'

Gibson writes about family news and that of his sister being unwell:

'the news of her becoming a mother I was not prepared to hear it may be for the best if he is not already Christened I hope she will call him "William" after her absent Brother ...'

He hopes the baby 'may never live to feel any of the troubles I have prayed over or perhaps may have to undergo'. He thanks his parents for their kindness, family good times, and for their thoughtfulness towards Maria his wife. He continues, 'I hope soon to see her in this country' but is surprised she hasn't replied to his last letter. Her journey might be made easier by the possible assistance of his master, James Thorneloe, as Thorneloe's mother is about to travel to Hobart Town and has indicated Maria might be able to travel with her. Gibson would like Maria to come but won't mention it again if she doesn't want to. However, if Maria joins him:

'I then shall feel a little more comfortable not having a friend in this country to whom I can unburden my mind when it is oppressed If I remember rightly 12 months was the stipulated period from my departure previous to her following me, that time is passed long since...'

He states that Maria does not need the governor's consent 'if she comes out without any assistance from the government. It is not required'. To this letter, James Thorneloe, Board of Assignment, added the following, dated 7 September 1833. He confirmed Gibson had been allowed to sleep out of Barracks within the last year, 'The first step to indulgence' and he had recently 'been placed upon the highest rate of pay allowed by the Government to writers of his class.' He added it would be good for Gibson to have his wife join him to support him and aid his improvement 'if his friends could contrive it…'

It's probable Maria did not join Gibson in Hobart soon after his letter, if ever. The Convict Conduct book shows that on 5 August 1833, Gibson was found in a public house after hours – he did not mention this in his letter to his father. On 17 May 1834, he was found out of hours in the company of a female servant which lead to him having to stay in the Prisoners' Barracks for six months. On 18 June 1834, still working as clerk for the Assignment board, he was found to put before the Principle Superintendent a paper assigning a servant to an 'improper person' claiming this was by order of the Assignment Board. This was not true and he was punished and removed from his job.

On 27 Sept 1834, Gibson refused to work in the Government Garden and his punishment included five days solitary confinement. On 31 January 1836, whilst he was a clerk again he was found out after hours; he was reprimanded. On 11 May 1840, he was in a public house whilst a card game was being played. The Conduct Book also carries a note of the Gaoler's Report which states he'd been convicted before, in England, in addition to the conviction for which he was transported. He received a conditional pardon in May 1843.

Chapter 10

Bodies
Murderers and the Resurrection Men

U nder the 1752 Murder Act, those found guilty of murder in England or Wales were to be hanged two days after sentencing, or three days if sentencing had taken place on a Friday. This was amended in 1834: a minimum of two Sundays had to elapse and it was increased again in 1868 to three Sundays. In Scotland, the time allowed between the two events was more generous, and depended on the location of the trial.

There were only a small number of options available to buy the prisoner time. An interjection by the defence counsel after a guilty verdict had been announced but before a sentence was passed down, could be used to claim an error had occurred. However, a 'writ of error' was expensive and delaying a sentence in any way meant petitioning for mercy could not take place because a sentence had not been pronounced.

Once sentencing had occurred, there was very little opportunity for a petition to be sent, although for women, successful proof of pregnancy would lead to a respite until after the child's birth. In such cases, it was not unusual for the respite, over time, to become a pardon.

With such a finite fate for those found guilty of murder and a growing unease surrounding the use of capital punishment, edges were sometimes blurred at the trial. Juries could return a partial verdict, finding the prisoner guilty of only an element of the charge, or of a similar but lesser offence, for example, manslaughter. Prisoners often pleaded insanity.

Duelling was still widespread in the 1820s but became less popular during the following decade as public opinion turned against the practice. Although those firing the shot might be charged with murder, they were often found guilty of manslaughter.

Under the 1752 Murder Act, the bodies of executed murderers were either sent to surgeons for anatomical research or 'hung in chains'. A murderer's body could only be buried if it had been sent first to the surgeons.

Elizabeth Jeffray (or **Elisabeth Jaffery**) had pleaded not guilty at Glasgow Circuit Court in 30 April 1838 when charged with the murders of Ann Newal (Ann Carl) and Hugo Monro, who had been poisoned with arsenic. The jury found Jeffray guilty and although they recommended mercy, she was sentenced to death; a date of execution was set for 21 May. Also known by the surname of Nicklson or Shafto, Elizabeth Jeffray was 33 (or 36) years old and the wife of Francis Jeffray, a miner.

Both of Jeffray's alleged victims were her fellow residents in Carluke, Lanarkshire, and her crimes had taken place the previous October. In the case of Ann Newal, Jeffray's elderly neighbour, the prisoner was adjudged to have mixed arsenic with meal, water and whisky and told Newal the mixture was medicine. With regards to Monro, Jeffray's lodger, she had first mixed arsenic in to his porridge, then two days later, with rhubarb.

Because of Ann Newal's age there were no immediate suspicions surrounding her death, but that of Monro, a labourer, was a different matter. The court was told how Jeffray had pushed for early burials for both Newal and Monro, and the bodies, once raised, were found to contain arsenic. Jeffray had recently obtained arsenic but when she claimed it had been to kill an infestation of rats, she was not believed - none of the witnesses had seen rats there.

The Broadsheet published by John Muir of Glasgow on the day of her execution claimed that Jeffray owed Monro £5 which she was unable to repay and this was thought the only motive for the crime. Neighbours claimed that Jeffray might have been ousting Monro in order to let his room to a more 'productive lodger' whilst the Deputy Advocate put forward the theory that Jeffray had used Newal as practice for poisoning Monro, because there seemed no other reason for Jeffray to murder her.

Petitions in support of Jeffray were sent to the Home Secretary, Lord John Russell. One, undated, was signed by Jeffray and twelve jury members and claimed that the evidence against her was circumstantial and:

> 'did not convince the whole of the Jury, who convicted her only by a majority and that even that majority concurred in a unanimous recommendation to mercy.'

They wrote that Jeffray had no motive and requested 'at least … a further enquiry'. A very similar petition was sent in the middle of May from 'merchants and other inhabitants of the city of Glasgow' but added:

> 'they are from a conscientious conviction opposed to capital punishments not only on the grounds of their impolicy and inefficiency, as a prevention of crime, but also on account of their repugnancy to the mild and beneficent spirit of the gospel.'

The covering letter noted there were 926 signatures to the petition, but they are not within the Home Office file. The Home Office annotation stated, 'Numerous signatures detatched' (ie. separated from the document).

A Carluke Minister and two Elders had written a character reference for Jeffray in early April 1838, and this was presented, confirming she was:

'... a member of the Relief Church in this place, and that up to the month of November last, nothing could be said against her [illegible] character – only that her attendance at Church was somewhat irregular – a circumstance which she attributed to indisposition.'

In early May, the judge Lord MacKenzie had forwarded notes of the evidence to the Lord Justice Clerk and did not recommend mercy. The Lord Justice Clerk, David Boyle, reported to the Home Secretary on 5 May and stated that Lord Mackenzie believed that:

'the jury were moved by compassion for the prisoners family, and dislike to a capital punishment in the case of circumstantial evidence'.

Boyle had reviewed the evidence and notes and concluded that 'I can entertain no doubt' Jeffray's guilt was established and added reasons, including 'her aversion to look upon' her victims in their agony, and her negligence 'to procure proper medical assistance'. He concluded that he concurred with the judgement of the circuit judge.

The petitions from Jeffray and her supporters were unsuccessful and Elizabeth Jeffray was executed.

On 11 September 1833, **Christian King** faced trial at Aberdeen Circuit Court, accused of the murder of her son. The boy had been born on 3 August and died two days later from wounds inflicted upon him. Around twenty-three years old, King was accused in her indictment of:

'wickedly and feloniously, with a post or piece of wood or some other such like weapon to the Prosecutor unknown... inflict upon the head and other parts of the person of a male child of which you, the said Christian King, had shortly before been delivered, one or more severe and mortal wounds, whereof the said child languished until... 5th day of August... [and died].'

The act had taken place in a privy at the house of King's employer, the Reverend Dr Daniel Dewar. The report in the *Morning Post*, London, 23 September 1833, described how King seemed greatly upset and kept her head down to hide her face when she was brought in to the court. King pleaded 'not guilty' but the trial judge, Lord MacKenzie, noted in his report to the Lord Justice Clerk, he considered as ill-founded the plea of *malum regimen*; such a plea attributes the cause of death to bad medical treatment rather than resulting from the defendant's actions. King was found guilty and sentenced to death, although the majority of the jurors recommended mercy. The day of execution was set for 7 October 1833 and King was returned to Aberdeen Tolbooth.

Christian King was born and raised in Reay, Caithness, the daughter of Benjamin King, an English ploughman, and his wife. The family were respectable, Benjamin King having been Kirk Officer for sixteen years by the time his daughter's trial took place. Christian King had worked as a cook for the Sinclair family in Thurso for approximately twelve months before the Sinclair family moved south to Torquay for the winter. From 11 April 1832 until 10 December the same year, she was in the employ of Kenneth and Janet Monro, the landlord and landlady at the Tongue Inn, Sutherland, before living with her father in Reay over the winter. King's sister heard of a vacancy at Albyn Place, Aberdeen, working for the Reverend Dr Daniel Dewar DD, the Principal of Marischal College. She told King of the opportunity and although she was reluctant to go there at first, Christian was eventually persuaded and began her employment in Aberdeen around 11 June 1833.

It was a few weeks into her service with Dr and Mrs Dewar that Mrs Dewar started to suspect King was pregnant. In the judge's notes, Lord MacKenzie recorded that Mrs Dewar claimed she asked King about this on both 13 and 15 July as far as she remembered. On each occasion, King denied it, first saying that it would be bad behaviour for her to come to work in that condition and on the second occasion that she would pledge it was not the case. Dr Dewar's suspicions were also aroused because of what the judge in his notes recorded as Christian's 'bulky appearance'.

Showing signs of sickness, King maintained she had a bowel complaint. On Saturday 3 August, the family and other servants went on an outing to the seaside and left King alone in the house. On their return, they found her looking very ill and Dr Keith was sent for. King was observed by the family and servants going back and forth to the privy several times.

With suspicions high, the privy was checked and a baby was discovered to have been pushed down it. The boy was badly scratched and bruised but alive. Near the privy, a post was found sticking in the ground, over four feet in length, and a second piece of wood was discovered, around eight inches long, with signs of blood. King was apprehended and brought before William Watson, Sheriff-Substitute of Aberdeenshire.

On 12 August, William Keith and John M. Campbell, surgeons, gave a report of the child's condition. They had been requested to attend Doctor Dewar's House on the evening of 3 August between six and seven o'clock and attended a 'newly born infant...a healthy and full grown male child'. They found the baby's body to have been 'generally much abused and scratched especially about the head and face'. The two doctors dressed the wounds and gave the baby to Mrs Goodall, a wet-nurse, at around 8 o'clock that evening. The child was strong and lively but he died two days later.

Christian King's respectable former character, her youth and the fact the murder did not appear pre-meditated but took place whilst she was extremely anxious, drew much sympathy from those she knew, as well as others. The Sinclairs wrote with certificates in her favour, both before and after her trial. One sent from Alexander Sinclair, confirmed that she worked 'very much to my wife's satisfaction as an excellent servant, and was very kind and affectionate to the children'. Another was sent from William Sinclair, now residing in London. Miss B.M.G. Sinclair, living in Edinburgh, also confirmed King's good character during her employment with the family and throughout September the Sinclairs continued to express their support.

On 6 September 1833, the Monros stated that at the beginning of her employment King had 'served faithfully and without suspicion attached to her moral character' but in the last month that changed when:

> '... rumours of impropriety of conduct between her and a Doctor Grant, then a lodger with us, not being satisfactorily explained to us, we parted with her. However she was very kind and affectionate to the children.'

It was undersigned by the Minister of Tongue.

Kings' neighbours in Reay wrote of her good character, as did David Mackay, minister, and the Clerk and Elders of Reay. They confirmed she 'conducted herself soberly, honestly and industriously' whilst serving at the Manse for twelve months, and 'gave full satisfaction'. The supporting certificates were sent to the Home Secretary in a covering letter from Alexander Bannerman, MP for Aberdeen and Chancellor of the Jury; he would continue to be the conduit through which representation was made.

A petition was sent in her support from 194 'Proprietors, Freeholders, Justices of the Peace, Tenants, Householders and others' from Aberdeen, including Daniel Dewar, King's employer and those of local advocates, merchants, bankers and seven members of the jury. A note points out that thirteen jury members concurred with the recommendation for mercy, but some had left Aberdeen after the trial and so could not sign the petition. Lord Sutherland and his mother petitioned on two occasions, asking for King's sentence to be mitigated. Mercy was requested by David Craigie from Edinburgh. Mr W. Innes wrote from Sandside, forwarding a copy of the recommendation of mercy by the jurors.

The strength needed to push the pole into the ground or into the child, was much debated. Charles Neaves, the prisoner's Counsel, forwarded letters from five doctors in Aberdeen who testified that it was possible for children to be born in a state of suspended animation.

In her declaration and petition in mid-September, Christian King admitted she had had a 'guilty connexion' with a man at the Tongue Inn, and that he was 'an individual considerably above her rank'. Knowing she was pregnant, she had been reluctant to go to work for the Dewars, but later complied. When the time to give birth arrived, she had intended to go missing, have the child and return to work saying she had lost her way. It also appears she intended to contact the father regarding maintenance for the child.

She stated she had made clothes for the child and had gone to visit her sister with the hope that her sister would then accompany her back to the Dewars, during which time she would explain her situation, but her sister's husband had taken her there instead. King said the child slipped down the privy and she thought it was dead because it wasn't crying. She used the stick, she claimed, to try and get it to the privy door and she was 'not conscious of using any violence'. She planned to return to the child within a few hours and take it to someone who could care for it.

Daniel Dewar wrote to Alexander Bannerman, with new evidence; significantly it was learnt King had been badly advised before her trial, a fact confirmed by William Watson, Sheriff-Substitute of Aberdeen. No evidence of mitigating circumstances therefore had been put before the court.

As a result of the new evidence, Lord MacKenzie opined that it was possible King had not intended to murder her son. David Boyle, Lord Justice Clerk, reported on the case and suggested mitigation of the sentence might be appropriate. As a result, King's execution was respited and on 30 September William Watson wrote to the Home Secretary, Viscount Melbourne acknowledging receipt of the order to that effect.

On 5 October 1833, two days before King was due to be executed, a pardon was prepared, on condition that she was transported for life.

Christian King was transported to New South Wales on the *Numa* in December 1833, arriving there the following June. During the voyage, she was treated by the ship's surgeon and superintendent, Edward F. Bromley. He notes in his medical journal that she was put on the sick list on 30 January 1834 and discharged, 'cured' on 8 February. She had been suffering from 'cynanche tonsillaris' – inflammatory sore throat.

New South Wales records show, after applying for tickets of leave in both Sydney and Windsor, she was granted a conditional pardon on 8 July 1854.

On 21 September 1838, **Henry Webber** and **John Young** were tried at the Old Bailey accused of the murder of Charles Flower Mirfin (or Murfin) the previous month. Webber and Young were two of five men due to stand trial for Mirfin's murder; the third, **Edward Delves Broughton** did not appear in court, his counsel's absence being given as a reason for his non-attendance; he was tried the following February. A fourth man, Francis Lionel Eliot, had disappeared and the fifth man was unidentified. All had been involved in a duel on Wimbledon Common in which Mirfin had been killed by Eliot's shot. Eliot was indicted for being a principle in the first degree and the others, principles in the second degree. It seems two other men were charged with being accessories.

Both Webber and Young were found guilty and death recorded. In entries for 21 September 1838, The Newgate Register of Prisoners describes Henry Webber as twenty-four years old, 5ft 10in tall and from Bloomsbury, London. Young was a 26-year-old from Putney, who was 5ft 8in tall.

From his cell in Newgate, Henry Webber petitioned the Queen and the Home Secretary, Lord John Russell. His petition centred on the fact that although he and Young were indicted for 'aiding and abetting in the said duel', neither man acted as second to the duellists. Webber stressed he had not been involved or connected in the initial quarrel between Mirfin and Elliot, the result of which was the duel. He added, 'nor did Petitioner in any wise forward or promote the duel between the parties.' In fact, he maintained, he had:

'exerted himself to the utmost of his ability – being acquainted with both the parties – to prevent a hostile meeting and with the view and the view alone of effecting a reconciliation did Prisoner assent to accompany the said Francis Lionel Eliot in the carriage hired by him to the Common.'

He added that whilst he had known Mirfin for some time, he had only known Eliot for two months.

According to Webber's petition, Eliot was unwilling to meet with Mirfin in a hostile encounter and had 'positively refused till provoked by the threat of being posted as a Coward…' Eliot had continued to hope the duel would be averted up to the last moment and had persuaded Webber to accompany Mirfin because Webber knew Mirfin well and could influence him 'to affect an arrangement of the difference'. Webber tried his utmost to do so but Mirfin demanded a written apology from Eliot which Eliot 'positively refused' to do although, according to Webber, Eliot did however affirm he would apologise verbally.

The duel had taken place around 6 o'clock in the evening of 22 August. Webber stated that after the first shot he tried to bring about a reconciliation and 'entreated and implored' Mirfin not to demand a second. When he found it impossible to make Mirfin take his advice, Webber walked away. As he was leaving, he heard the second shot and when he looked around he saw by Mirfin's gestures that he had been wounded. Joining the others, he was with Mirfin when he 'breathed his last'.

Webber claimed he was wholly unaware that he was committing a crime through the role he played maintaining that he had a clear conscience, using 'all means of expostulation and entreaty' to stop the duel going ahead. He explained he had no witnesses to speak for him at the trial because all those who could clarify his role in the event had been indicted themselves. The only excluded person was Mr [Dr Edman] Scott and:

> '…[he] admitted that he was so engrossed with the loading of the pistols and the arrangement for the duel that he did not even observe whether Petitioner was actually present or not at the firing.'

Webber stated the judge, Mr Justice Vaughan, told the jury they must consider whether the defendants were 'aiding and abetting' Mirfin and Eliot when the shot that killed Mirfin was fired. If the defendant interceded or assisted or was close enough to render assistance, then he was to be found 'guilty'. Webber claimed that the judge was 'intimating to the jury that it was a question of considerable doubt.'

Webber was found guilty and death recorded, but, claimed Webber, it was:

> 'with an intimation from the Learned Judge that such sentence would be Commuted to a term of imprisonment.'

The judge also advised Webber to petition for mercy.

Webber assured the Home Secretary he was not trying to 'seek to justify the practice of Duelling either as a moral or a legal act…' but that it had been widely adopted by all classes of society, and imprisonment did not usually follow.

As further reasons for clemency, Webber cited that he was only twenty-five years old and:

'has just commenced business on his own account, he is now utterly ruined, his prospects in life if not destroyed at all events most severely blighted and worse than all he has brought on his parents the unutterable anguish of seeing their son tried at the Old Bailey as a murderer and sentence to death recorded against him.'

The prosecutor, Mirfin's brother, had recommended mercy and, Webber continued, if mercy was shown to him he would use the rest of his life to express his gratitude 'by uniform obedience'. The letter carries the Home Office annotation, 'Nil'.

On 24 September, John Young petitioned the Home Secretary, from Newgate, using the same arguments in his defence as used by Webber. Like Webber, he claimed that no one had been imprisoned for duelling as far as he understood and the prosecutor's counsel had recommended mercy. Young claimed that he had already been affected by the confinement and diet within prison, although he had only been there a short time. In addition:

'Petitioners mother, from the conviction of your Petitioner, is in a dangerous state of health arising from your Petitioners confinement under this charge.'

The same month, the Home Secretary received an anonymous letter from Exeter, which is in Webber's case file:

'You are a parent you know not what your children may be obliged to do as to their honour. Take compassion in those unhappy Boys you have so harshly sentenced as to the late Duel and do Justice to Rich and Poor.'

Also included in Webber's file is a cutting from *The Times* newspaper of 1 October 1838. It carried a correction to a previous report in which the paper had stated 'hard labour' had been part of the sentences for Webber and Young, but this had been erroneous. The article also asked the Government to consider the wisdom and justice of giving Webber and Young more than a token punishment. The article pointed out there was a difference between the law and the custom regarding duelling, adding that most distinguished men had been willingly involved in a duel in some capacity.

The lengthy article, which has no writer's name attached, suggested the harsh sentence might be justified by some people as an attempt to bring an end to duelling, but if that was the desired outcome then fair means should be used. This case had demonstrated an apparent change of response to 'two lads' who were only spectators at an event the type of which was usually regarded as innocent, praiseworthy and 'under given circumstances, positively indispensable…'

Two days later, the paper carried a second lengthy article in response to another newspaper's misrepresentation of *The Times* original article. In this response, the paper stated *The Times* was concerned that the misrepresentation might harm Webber and Young's case. It continued to express support for the men and hoped their severe sentences would be reduced by the Government.

The Newgate Register of Prisoners shows entries for both Webber and Young of 'death recorded, 1 Year House of Correction without labour, last month solitary'. They were sent to Guildford Gaol on 6 October 1838.

John Young petitioned the Home Secretary from Guildford Gaol. Again he stated that he had been found guilty as a principal, but he was only present as a spectator, adding that he has 'suffered much both in Body and Mind from the time of his conviction and sentence…' and if freed, would be guided by his family who were suffering from their son's 'folly and inexperience'. The petition is undersigned by seventeen signatories who asked for clemency due to the prisoner's youth and prospects, his contrition and for his family, particularly his parents, who are deeply ashamed by the actions of their son. The first signatory is that of Christthomas Robinson, a curate at St Mary's, Putney, and others include Richard Alsager, MP for Surrey Eastern Division; Frederick Hodgson MP; the Earl of Ripon; G.G. De H. Larpent, Magistrate for Surrey.

On 8 April 1839, the Home Office replied to Christthomas Robinson. Young had been granted a pardon on condition of one month solitary confinement. On 9 April, Robinson wrote to Lord John Russell acknowledging receipt of his 'despatch' and telling the Home Secretary:

'I have communicated the indulgence to the Parties most in [illegible] in it and I beg to thank you most sincerely on their behalf as well as on my own for the very kind and prompt manner in which you have been pleased to answer the prayer of an Petition.'

Interestingly, a Home Office memorandum of late September 1838 states that John Young's father had brought petitions:

'I told him that the Jury having given their verdict upon the evidence and the judge having recommended a commutation of sentence, I could not do otherwise than recommend to the Crown such commutation. That it might be on a question hereafter whether a pardon might be granted to do away the civil penalties of felony (My present intention is to remit the last fortnight of solitary confinement and grant a free pardon after 11 ½ months of confinement).'

The note is unsigned. Clearly, Young's sentence was reduced further as was that of Webber.

Edward Delves Broughton was 22-years-old when he was taken into custody. He was 5ft 8in tall and a labourer from Bath, according to the Newgate Register of Prisoners. He pleaded guilty when tried in February 1839 and received the same sentence as Webber and Young. Broughton was sent to Guildford Gaol on 27 February 1839.

Edward Broughton and his supporters petitioned and argued he should only serve the same sentence as the others accessories. On 29 July 1839, his sentence was reduced to 8 months imprisonment.

Mirfin's friend, Dr Edman Scott, had acted as surgeon at the duel but had not been tried with the others. According to reports in *The Gentleman's Magazine* and *The Annual Register or a View of the History and Politics of the Year*, Scott was bound over in his own recognizances for £300, to appear when required to do so. Broughton claimed in his petitions that Scott had managed the duel and thwarted any attempt at reconciliation between the parties. He had also been the main prosecution witness. *The Gentleman's Magazine* and *The Annual Register* also reported that Eliot had fled 'abroad', as Broughton had initially done. The original incident which lead to the duel concerned a clash of the men's carriages in Epsom some months prior to the duel.

From the late eighteenth century, the study of anatomy had become central to medical training and research, but as the demand for bodies increased, the source of their supply became an issue of great concern to the general public. The 1752 Murder Act had supplemented existing official sources for surgeons, allowing the bodies of those executed for murder to be available for dissection, but as the number of medical students grew, so did the trade in body-snatching. The Anatomy Act, which received the Royal Assent on 1 August 1832, was designed to calm the fears of the public and regulate the supply to schools. The Act allowed 'unclaimed' bodies to be dissected, for example those who had died in workhouses or hulk prison ships, without family or friends who were able to bury them.

In early May 1834, less than two years after the Anatomy Act came in to force, James Somerville gave evidence to the Parliamentary Select Committee on Medical Education, regarding the current state of the anatomy schools and the Act's effect upon them. Dr Somerville was the first Inspector for England and Wales appointed under the Act to regulate the schools of anatomy on behalf of the Home Secretary, with Dr Craigie appointed for Scotland. Somerville was well positioned to be appointed inspector; as he told the Select Committee when questioned, he had been attached to Dr Hunter's theatre in Great Windmill Street, London and was familiar with the other schools in the London area. In addition, he had knowledge of European schools, having been a student in Paris.

When asked his opinion, Somerville stated that prior to the Act, the anatomical schools had been 'at the mercy' of those who traded in exhuming and then selling bodies. Since the Act's enforcement, the bodies were being received in a fresher condition and the expense was 'moderate', being only the cost of their transportation to the school and their subsequent interment. Supply had been good so a larger number of students had better facilities; it had only been the mild season which had affected supply.

Somerville's local officers had reported factors which would have an increasing impact; the poor were enjoying improved conditions leading to better general health and higher employment meant fewer people had to leave their dead relatives unclaimed. Bodies had been treated with great propriety and decorum he said, adding he knew of only one instance – in Cambridge – out of 1000 in the metropolis and 200 in the wider country, where there had been any 'untoward circumstance'. He was sure those schools outside of London, which had previously supplied themselves from inside London, were also being brought into line.

The effect of the Act had been to stop the practice of exhumation, Somerville stated, adding that he knew there was not a single case in the criminal calendar of a charge for disinterring bodies. Now the Act ensured sufficient supply, at moderate cost, exhuming bodies illegally had lost its financial appeal for the criminals. However, work was still having to be undertaken to ensure schools had a fair distribution based on their number of pupils. Despite initial agreements to do this, some schools were still using their local influence to gain a larger supply to the disadvantage of other establishments. Maintenance of supply did become a problem in many places, resulting in the amalgamation of some schools.

The strength of public opinion with regard to keeping bodies safely interred, is evidenced in the case of **William Cooke**, a surgeon. At the Epiphany Sessions for the City and County of Exeter in 1827, William Cooke was indicted:

'for breaking and entering in to a grave in the churchyard at the parish church at Saint David... and taking and carrying away the Dead Body of one Elizabeth Taylor.'

In a separate Bill of Felony he was charged with stealing the 'wearing apparel' the body was clad in, although it was acknowledged these were of very little value. Bail was set at £200 and two separate sureties of £100.

In his petition to William Sturges Bourne, the Home Secretary, dated 26 May 1827, Cooke explained:

'That from the violent Prejudices excited against your Petitioner in that city on account of these offences, your Petitioner found it necessary to apply to the Court of Kings Bench for a Writ of Certiorari, for the removal of the said indictments and they were then accordingly removed into the said Court of Kings Bench, and finally sent down for trial *nisi prius*, at the last Assize for the County of Devon.'

When tried at the Devon Assizes the jury deliberated for several hours and found Cooke guilty of the first charge. He was acquitted on the second charge when no evidence was offered supporting the Prosecution.

Cooke informed the Home Secretary that he had returned to England from France in October 1826 where he had been following his profession as a surgeon. He had gone to Exeter intending not only to work there but because of his feelings of duty, interest and a love of science to which he had devoted himself. He had given a course of anatomical lectures for free which were, he claimed, well and civilly attended, and he realised he might have to show a dissection of a real body for a lecture concerning musculature. However, mindful not to risk upsetting those who might attend the lectures, or his fellow citizens Cooke had arranged for a body to be supplied from a considerable distance away from the event.

Unfortunately, Cooke's arrangements did not turn out as planned and his hoped for demonstration aid did not come to fruition. With a lecture announced for 9 November 1826, Cooke very reluctantly approached Giles Yarde, a labourer and former grave digger, to enquire if he could help supply a 'subject' and, helpfully, Yarde knew of a forthcoming funeral. Cooke and Yarde agreed terms and to remove and cover the body respectfully, fill in the grave and return it to its former condition. Cooke stressed that he did not want to cause any distress or worry anyone about 'the safety of Places of interment in the vicinity of Exeter.'

Around 4 o'clock in the morning of 9 November, the body of Elizabeth Taylor was removed and taken to Cooke's house. He told the Home Secretary that he had emphasised to Yarde again the need for decency and paid him extra to ensure that the grave was filled in properly and made good. He claimed that he had no reason to believe this had not happened. However, the following morning the grave was found:

> 'in a state of disorder and exposure which not only left no room to doubt of the fact which had taken place but was naturally calculated to excite strong feelings of disgust and indignation at any person who might be presumed intentionally to have occasioned so indecent a spoiliation.'

Cooke fully regretted his actions, he wrote, the result of which was not his intention. Yarde was indicted, seemingly with the same charge.

Cooke stated in his petition that the prosecutor pursued him 'with the most unrelenting severity…' Cooke managed to persuade the magistrate to agree to set bail at £200 and two sureties of £100 each. This, he claimed, was unusual given the small value of the articles in question.

Cooke claimed that his future prospects in his profession had been damaged, especially any chance of working in the local area because he had upset the local people. He recounted how he had had his feelings 'severely harassed' and had been put to great expense. He explained that he was a husband and father and was well-educated. When his case had come before Kings Bench on 17 May, he had submitted good character references from other people in his profession, citing Dr Blackall, W. Tucker and Mr Abernethy. The fine of £200 he believed to be severe and with the expense of defending himself he had been involved 'in much difficulty and distress'. He asked for the fine to be re-paid.

Cooke received support from John Abernethy, who petitioned the Home Secretary on 2 June 1827. Abernethy was principal surgeon at St Bartholomew's Hospital until he retired on 24 July 1827. Writing from Bedford Row, London, he stated:

'Mr Cooke has been a very industrious and intelligent student of his profession and is a person of good character.'

Hoping to help Cooke's case, he explained that, when the offence was detected:

'great popular indignation was excited, his usual course of professional Business was interrupted, his mind distracted, his Time occupied in legal proceedings and attendance and dreading the effects of local prejudice, he removed the adjudication of his cause to the Court of Kings Bench.'

Because Cooke could not pay the fine:

'a gentleman, from humanity, advanced the money and saved him from imprisonment. His health having suffered very considerably he could not return to Exeter but is awaiting at a village in Devonshire, the result of his petition to Government for the Remission of this fine.'

The efforts of Cooke and Abernethy appear to be unsuccessful; the Home Office annotation reads 'Refused'.

John Williams was tried at the Middlesex Sessions on 11 April 1825, charged with stealing dead bodies from a churchyard. Found guilty, he was sentenced to six months with hard labour in the House of Correction for Middlesex. From his cell, the prisoner sent a petition to the Home Secretary, undated, in which he explained that before his indictment he was an under-gardener with several persons and always conducted himself with 'honesty and fidelity to his employer.'

As reasons for clemency he claimed that some time before he was imprisoned he:

'formed an attachment to one Mary Bowerman who is now pregnant by your Petitioner and likely to be delivered before the expiration of the term before which your Petitioner is imprisoned.'

Banns of marriage had been regularly published in the church of St Margaret, Westminster, and he was very anxious to marry before his child was born. Mary Bowerman:

> 'hath declared herself pregnant by John Williams... and hath become chargeable to the Parish of St Christopher Le Stocks in the City of London.'

The petition is undersigned by two churchwardens, William Grubb and Mr Coleman.

Unfortunately for John Williams, this petition was unsuccessful. The Home Office annotation, dated 2 July 1825, is 'Refused'.

In January 1832, seven months before The Anatomy Act gained its royal assent, **Isaac Hunt**, sometimes called Henry Hunt, or Isaac Henry Hunt, was tried at Gloucester Quarter Sessions for stealing a dead body. Found guilty, Hunt was sentenced to six months imprisonment in North Leach Gaol, Gloucestershire. But Hunt had not carried out the act for financial gain; he was a messenger servant of the Royal College of Surgeons in London. On 17 February 1832, Sir Astley Cooper, Council Member, former and future President, and Sergeant Surgeon to George IV, William IV and Victoria, had sent a letter to the Home Office. It is not certain to whom the letter was originally addressed, but writing from Conduit Street, he begins, 'I have a favour to beg of Lord Melbourne and yourself...' and seeks a reduction in Hunt's sentence. The letter explained this was Hunt's first offence and he had carried it out as a result of 'super abundant zeal' for the College having learnt the body was of 'extraordinary forms'. The letter added that many respectable gentlemen would give Hunt a good character. However, the Home Secretary did not change his mind, and the petition letter was marked as 'Nil'.

A petition followed in April 1832 from the Members of the Council of the Royal College of Surgeons, explaining again Hunt had learnt of the death of a person he considered would be a noteworthy and valuable specimen for the College museum. The body in question was that of John Cox of Oakridge in the parish of Bisley, Gloucestershire, who had died in October 1831. The letter described John Cox as not only very small but also 'singularly deformed'. Hunt had, however, acted without the sanction or knowledge of the College President in attempting to obtain it but, claimed the letter, 'solely with the view of promoting science'. As further reasons for mitigating the sentence, the letter stated that this was the only blot on Hunt's good character and

Hunt had already been confined some time before his trial. The letter was signed by Sir Astley Cooper, William Blizard, John P. Vincent, James Briggs, Benjamin Travers, Charles Bell, Henry Earle and B.C. Brodie.

All the signatories, along with others, had written to Viscount Melbourne on 10 December 1831 as part of the pressure being put by the RCS which would help bring about the Anatomy Act. In the letter of 10 December 1831, which is published in the Parliamentary Papers for the Session 6 December 1831 to 16 August 1832, the writers had pointed out that under Common Law at that point, anyone who was dissecting a human body, or:

> 'even has it in his possession for any other purpose than that of burial, is guilty of a misdemeanour, unless it be the body of a male-factor hanged for murder.'

The writers go on to point out that should the student make a mistake later in practice, as a result of insufficient anatomical knowledge, they could have civil action against them.

The petition on Hunt's behalf stated that he was detected in his attempt and committed to the gaol in Gloucester in order to be tried at the Sessions which would ensue.

The letter from Sir Astley Cooper and supporting Royal College of Surgeons signatories was answered by the Home Office on 28 April 1832. The annotation from the Home Office noted Hunt was 'to be remitted at the end of four months'. The remission was prepared, for the king to sign, on 7 May 1832.

In November 1832, after the Anatomy Act had been passed, **George Arnold** was tried at Middlesex Sessions, on the charge of disinterring a dead body. Found guilty, he was sentenced to nine months imprisonment in the House of Correction, Cold Bath Fields. His case came to the attention of James Somerville. On 19 December, with the Anatomy Act less than five months old, James Somerville wrote to the Home Secretary from 5 Saville Row, London. He stated:

> 'Your Lordship thought it necessary that a prosecution should take place in the present case for the purpose of satisfying the public that government is determined to put down the old practice of unburying bodies, and to give full effect to the recent Act relative to the practice of Anatomy.

> 'This prosecution has I believe had a very good effect on satisfy-
> ing the public feeling, and from all the information I have been able
> to collect after diligent enquiry, I am satisfied that the old practice
> is at an end, and that those who once practised this business follow
> it no longer.'

Somerville added that he had 'made very particular enquiry respecting the
character and habits of the prisoner' and from these enquiries had concluded
that Arnold did not steal bodies for business, this being the first time he was
involved in such a thing, 'induced to do so by a man of the name of Phillips
who has given up his former practice'. In citing reasons for clemency,
Somerville stated Arnold's father, a coal merchant in Milton, was a very
respectable man and Arnold's mother was dying. Arnold's father had visited
his son in jail, and Somerville had done the same and had 'been struck with
the appearance of sincere repentance and concern at all that has happened.
There is no doubt that he was made the dupe of Phillips…' Arnold's father
intended to give his son immediate employment on his release. Somerville
suggested this case was entitled to:

> 'a merciful consideration in so much as it is well known that these
> men were encouraged and brought up to their business by the
> Anatomical Teachers.'

Remission was prepared for Arnold on 20 December 1832, the day after
Somerville wrote his letter.

Chapter 11

Words from Newgate Prison, London

Newgate Prison was the primary prison for London and held many categories of prisoners including those who had been committed and were awaiting trial at the Old Bailey; those who had been convicted and awaiting removal to their place of imprisonment or the next stage of their fate; prisoners tried and found guilty in other courts, serving short sentences; debtors. Mayhew and Binny categorise it as a 'Detentional Prison', a sub-category of 'Criminal Prisons'.

After its destruction in the Gordon Riots of 1780, Newgate had been rebuilt. The reconstruction was finished in 1783, with its design unaltered from the previous reconstruction completed five years earlier. The prison was based on three quadrangles of wards, each with their own central courtyard in which the prisoners took exercise. Male prisoners, female prisoners and debtors were confined in separate quadrangles. Those who could afford to pay for more comfortable accommodation were imprisoned in the state area.

Newgate was adjacent to the Old Bailey court and, from November 1783, hangings were held in front of the prison when those at Tyburn ceased, this change seemingly 'at the suggestion of [John] Howard, from philanthropic motives, to do away with the unseemly processions to Tyburn.'[1]

Edward Duncombe was a newspaper agent and publisher from Fleet Street and Middle Row, London, who was tried for selling prints of an obscene nature or an obscene libel. Found guilty, he was committed to Newgate for six months by the Court of Kings Bench in Easter Term, 1836. He petitioned the Home Secretary twice in July 1836, complaining about his treatment by the governor and the ensuing effects on his health.

In his first petition, dated 15 July, Duncombe describes how, on arrival at Newgate, he was placed in 'Chapel Yard' which he says he is informed is the 'place... appropriated to Kings Bench prisoners.' He continues that a few days later he was moved with two other prisoners, bankrupts, into the 'State Room'. Here he 'was allowed my provisions to be sent in to me by my wife'. 'About a fortnight' later he was moved to a room:

'entirely by myself the door of which was allowed to be open certain portions of the day to enable me to walk in the Yard for the benefit of my health, get water etc but all my provisions were stopped from coming in to me and many different orders at times given respecting me.'

He tells Lord John Russell how on 11 July 1836, Mr W.W. Cope, the prison governor, gave an order:

'unknown to me that my door should be kept closed except from 6–8 am while the room was being cleaned.' [However, the following day, the Governor ordered] 'that my door should be kept entirely closed and should not be left open for one minute in the twenty four hours'.

Duncombe continues to complain about the number and nature of the 'capricious orders' of W.W. Cope, including being 'put up in a single room with a dirty water closet attached the effluence from which at this season of the year is peculiarly annoying'. He alleges he is being 'singled out' and men convicted of 'Disgusting and Unnatural crimes are not subjected to what I am…' He was sent two newspapers but the parcel was opened and these withheld from him.

On 29 July 1836, Duncombe wrote again to Lord John Russell and refers back to his earlier letter. Unsure whether or not the Home Secretary has been in communication with the 'authorities', Duncombe encloses a copy of letter he sent to Mr Cope and states Mr Cope has yet to acknowledge it:

'My Lord I am now suffering greatly in my health from my being confined to one room without my door ever being left unlocked as other doors are or being allowed to walk when my health permits. My Lord I have not now been out to walk for three weeks, but since I wrote to your Lordship Mr Cope has ordered that I walk in the "Transport Yard" from eight o'clock until two but ill or well my Lord if I do not walk then I must not walk at all! I must walk the whole time the same time Mr Cope gave that order he also placed in the yard (where they never were allowed before) two men and a boy, who are here for trial for beastly assaults consequently my Lord I declined to avail myself of his order My Lord Mr Cope has stated to me that he cannot allow me to walk in the yard belonging to my room because he must keep men and boys separate, yet my Lord he now allows six men to walk in the yard every day with the boys and a boy slept for 22 nights in the mens room.'

Duncombe mentions that he is being treated for an illness by the prison surgeon, Mr Macmurdo, and although he gives no details of this illness he claims that the governor is fully aware of it:

'and yet, My Lord, I was locked up by his order on Monday last the 25th inst from half past ten in the morning until eight in the evening nearly ten hours without seeing an individual or being able to procure the Medicine that the surgeon had ordered me the day before (this is the second day I have been kept locked without my medicine) In fact My Lord from the third of July to the twelfth I never saw Mr Cope at all, except on the Saturday for about two minutes in company with the Sheriff Lawson when they refused to hear what I had to say and immediately left the room My Lord I am quite aware of the power I have to contend against in this appeal to Your Lordship (Mr Cope having told me that "if you are not quiet he would make it more severe for me") but still I do appeal with confidence as vehemently I believe that however humble the supplicant to Your Lordship he will not appeal in vain!'

He offered to order his solicitor to forward an affidavit 'as to the truth of my statement' and added that he has written three letters to the Sheriff and received one reply, a copy of which he encloses. Duncombe asks the Home Secretary for his advice and direction.

The Sheriff's letter to which Duncombe referred was dated 18 July 1836, replying to Duncombe's letter of 12 July. In it, John Lawson states that:

'… the Sherriffs have no desire to impose on you any restrictions that are not thought necessary while you are under confinement in Newgate.

'You must be well aware that in such a place it will be necessary for you to submit to much personal inconvenience. I would recommend to you the propriety of making your situation as little [illegible] as circumstances will allow.'

He assures Duncombe that Mr Cope and the Sheriffs:

'are disposed to afford you every opportunity in their power to take exercise in the yard on all suitable occasions.'

In a copy letter to W.W. Cope dated 21 July 1836, Duncombe complains of Cope's conduct towards him:

'You sir have given <u>sixteen different</u> orders varying the rules (as applied to me <u>individually</u>) within the short space of three months, in one instance an order was given before me in my room and upon going out to walk within ten minutes, you had unknown to me rescinded it again Sir On Monday 11th inst you without giving me the least notice assigning any cause gave an order that <u>My</u> door should be locked up at eight oclock and kept closed until two, and then I might walk from 2 to 5, but you also gave an order that ill or well that if I did not walk <u>at Two</u> I was not to walk at all! On Tuesday 12th inst you Sir came up to my room door accompanied by Mr Newman about ¼ before eight in the morning when the man Griffith by whom <u>you</u> had during the whole time of my imprisonment, sent my bread, meat, soup etc to me, had <u>that minute</u> brought in my bread <u>as usual</u>, when you came to the door <u>which was wide open</u> and immediately ordered me to be locked up the <u>whole of every 24 hours! for what? for speaking to the man yourself had sent to me?!</u> But by such order implying that I was doing something improper and the very unusual order you have subsequently given respecting me (not <u>one of which is applied to any other man in the prison</u>) one of which is that no man should be allowed to speak to me, or have the slightest communication, has given rise to a <u>suspicion</u> that I <u>must</u> have done something very horrible and which I beg to say that I have a right to have cleaned up You sir have also given an order that the Turnkey shall unlock <u>my door at seven and wait in the room while it is cleaned</u> to this no other man is subject through the whole prison my door being locked up again the moment it is <u>done!!</u>'

Duncombe complains his health is worsening through lack of medicine and exercise and adds that he's neither a felon nor a 'convict' and Cope has never had any issues with his conduct.

Despite Duncombe's claims of unfair treatment and that the conditions he was enduring were detrimental to his health, it would seem his sentence was not reduced; his petitions carry the Home Office annotation 'Nil'.

Chapter 12

'Personal'

'Keeping a Brothel' and 'Assault with intent to Rape' were misdemeanours and as such were tried in Petty Sessions and sometimes, though not often, at Courts of Quarter Sessions. This level of offence carried punishments including short terms of detention, sureties, fines, whipping, or a combination of these. Felonies were tried at Courts of Quarter Sessions and Courts of Assize, most felonies being capital and thus carrying the death penalty. Rape carried the death penalty until 1841.

Incidents of 'Indecent Exposure' were often dealt with in police courts and carried short terms of imprisonment. In 1836, when Edward Duncombe was accused of selling prints of an obscene nature or obscene libel he was tried at the Court of Kings Bench and, found guilty, was sentenced to six months in Newgate prison. (See Chapter 11)

An outing in the park for French national **Antoine Villicus** ended in a three month gaol sentence; he had been found guilty of indecent exposure in the enclosure at St James's Park, London. Villicus was tried at Westminster Police Court, Queen Square, where he was committed on 4 September 1838 under the name of 'Antoine Valleure', and sent to Westminster Bridewell.

Villicus, a tailor from Toulouse, had travelled to England with his family four months previously in order to find work. Around 36 years of age, he was married with two small children. He professed his innocence of the charge against him, claiming it was a case of mistaken identity.

Imprisoned, Villicus enlisted the help of his fellow countryman, the well-regarded M. Cabel. On 18 September, Cabel visited Joseph Hume MP who, after Cabel had left, immediately wrote to Lord John Russell, the Home Secretary. Describing M. Cabel as 'formerly one of the most distinguished' French Deputies, Hume recounted how Cabel had urged him to draw Lord John Russell's attention to the fact Villicus could not understand English. He had not understood the complaint or the witnesses' assertions and could not defend himself due to this lack of language skills. Of the magistrate at the Westminster Police Court, Hume added:

'I do not know whether Mr White is a master of the French language but I think every metropolitan magistrate should be a french scholar'.

M. Cabel wrote to Joseph Hume the following day, and a further, undated, letter followed. The letters, in French, are with the Home Office case papers.

On 21 September, Fox Maule, Under-Secretary of State for the Home Office, wrote to William A.A. White, the magistrate at the centre of the case, enclosing M. Cabel's letter. The next day, Joseph Hume wrote again to Lord John Russell asking about Villicus, who he referred to as:

'a poor French tailor who has been condemned by Mr White of the Police Office, as seems to me, without sufficient evidence…'

White replied from the Police Office, Queen Square, on 25 September 1838. To answer the questions about the event that took place, he enclosed the statement from the 'females' to whom Villicus was said to have exposed himself, remarking that Villicus appeared to have exposed himself more than once and that 'some gentlemen had been induced to assist in speaking to the police' about it.

St James's Park had been redesigned by John Nash in the 1820s and by the later years of the decade its formal character had been exchanged for a more naturalistic one with meandering paths and a lake. The enclosure in which Villicus' offence took place was opposite Horse Guards.

Copies of witness depositions from Elizabeth Marriott and Caroline Barber taken on 4 September 1838 were enclosed in White's reply to Fox Maule. Elizabeth Marriott lived at 43, Maiden Lane, Strand and was employed as a servant to Mr McCartney. She described how she was in the enclosure in St James's Park on the previous afternoon, sitting on the grass, and facing the Duke of York's monument. She was looking after several children and was being helped by young fellow-servant, Caroline Barber, who was carrying one of the children. At around 5 o'clock Elizabeth noticed Villicus behind a tree to her rear. He 'coughed very loud' and when Elizabeth looked around she 'saw him with his trousers undone.' She claimed Villicus 'exposed himself three or four times' and she'd seen him do the same thing the previous week in almost the same location. Elizabeth tried to find a policeman but having no luck she returned to the others. When a policeman passed by soon afterwards, she told him what she had seen and Villicus ran off.

Caroline Barber recounted how she saw Villicus behind some trees 'and he shook the trees and said, "Hi, Little Girl".' When she turned to look around she saw Villicus had his clothes unfastened 'and he showed me his private parts'. When Elizabeth went to get a policeman, Caroline claimed Villicus came out from the trees 'and laid down near me'. His clothes at this point were refastened.

Policeman No. 49A, James Eyton described how, the previous afternoon around half past five, he had acted on information given to him by three gentlemen and gone to the shrubbery in the enclosure. There he saw Villicus who, on noticing the policeman, sprang up and walked away. Constable Eyton followed, touched him on the shoulder and asked him 'how he came to insult the females'. According to Eyton's statement, Villicus denied it was him. When Eyton told Villicus he had to accompany the policeman to the police station Villicus, he said, replied, 'Me don't comprehend'. Eyton stated that it was not the first time he had seen Villicus in the park.

Countering Villicus' claim that he could not understand the complaint, evidence or defend himself because of his lack of English, White pointed out that Villicus had been accompanied by his friends and his employer, one acting as an interpreter, translating the evidence 'to him sentence by sentence'. The friend then conversed with Villicus and Villicus' answer was given in English. Villicus' defence, in the interpreter's words was that he was 'only making urine'.

White re-iterated that every care was taken that the prisoner would fully understand the complaint and the police had no doubt regarding his identity. Answering a grievance concerning access to the prisoner, White stated that he was:

> 'not aware of any application having been made by, nor of course of any refusal having been given to, his wife, as to seeing him, or for any other purpose, and on enquiry am told she never did apply.'

Villicus' friends made orders for admission to him but this seems to have stopped when:

> '... as I am informed applications were made by strangers which seemed to be made from mere curiosity, and likely to prove as unpleasant to himself as they would have proved inconvenient to the regulations of the prison.'

It is not clear from the Home Office notes whether Villicus' petitioning had an effect on reducing his sentence, but he was not the only person to have been charged with indecent exposure in St James's Park, who then petitioned the Home Office for mercy.

The previous September, **Charles Horwood**, a 34-year-old hot pressing assistant, received the same sentence of three months in Westminster Bridewell. He too had claimed he was innocent and had only stopped to urinate. Twenty-three employees of the Shakespeare Printing office in Pall Mall petitioned on his behalf, citing his previous good character, his long-standing employment record of twelve years at the printers and the fact that he had a pregnant wife and several children dependent upon him. It was claimed his was a case of mistaken identity and the real culprit ran away. There was only one witness to the act. The outcome of his petition is not noted.

Three months after Villicus' conviction, **Joseph Degouy**, a valet, was charged with the same offence in St James's Park. Although the court in which he stood trial is not mentioned in the petition sent from his master, Degouy received six weeks imprisonment in Westminster Bridewell. His master petitioned on 13 December citing as reasons for mercy that Degouy had only just arrived in England, possibly from France, and had been a trustworthy servant for sixteen years. He claimed that Degouy was unable to speak English and knew nothing of English laws. However, Degouy's master was leaving England soon and he assured the Home Office he would take Degouy with him and would not return. It's likely this was the most persuasive reason in securing the remission Degouy received two days later.

On 23 April 1836, **Matthew Reason**, a painter, stood trial for indecently exposing himself to Mrs Jane Evans of Old Brompton, London, the previous day. A warrant for his arrest had been issued by H. G. Codd JP. Found guilty, Reason received a sentence of two months imprisonment in Middlesex House of Correction, despite the fact that he claimed the victim was not convinced of his guilt. Shortly after he was committed, Reason petitioned the Home Office, supported by sixteen character witnesses. Among the reasons he offered to support his plea for clemency were that his pregnant wife and child were dependent upon him and he was at work when the crime happened. Unfortunately for Reason he was unable to procure witnesses in time to confirm this.

'My Lord, various attempts are being made to obtain the liberation of **Mary Stewart**, now confined for assisting in the violation of a young female; the pretence is ill health, tho' the fact is her health has improved under confinement. The whole case is well known, and should she be liberated by such unjust *Favors, the whole proceedings shall be in Public Papers.' Signed 'My Lord. Your Obedient Servant "a father" *Parties using her house, - of course a little interested, - Lords G – and A.'

So stated the anonymous letter sent to the Home Secretary, Lord John Russell, on 22 August 1838. Mary Stewart had been tried at the Middlesex Sessions of July that year, charged with keeping a brothel at 26, Portland Place, Charlotte Street, London, between 1 July 1837 and 22 May 1838. Stewart was no more than 38 years old and was suffering from breast cancer. She had also been accused of organising the rape of a virgin.

The prosecution had been brought by the London Society for the Suppression of Juvenile Prostitution who, according to an undated newspaper clipping from *The Times* in the Home Office petition file, wanted to end 'the abominable and horrible system which had been adopted by such persons as the defendant.' Stewart pleaded guilty to keeping a house of ill-fame but denied the 'aggravated circumstances' in the affidavit which the Society had submitted. The newspaper reported the defence counsel hoped that the Court would take into account her illness, which it acknowledged would almost certainly soon prove fatal. The Chairman remarked that if the details in the affidavit were true, Stewart:

> 'might think herself extremely fortunate that she had not been executed as a felon… it was a case in which the severest vengeance of the law was loudly demanded'.

The girl who had given the affidavit was Martha, or Patty, Bull.

Questions were put to Patty Bull by Mr Sergeant Adams, the Chairman of the Sessions, and her statement of replies is within the Home Office file. She told him she would be seventeen next January and claimed that she first met Mary Stewart when looking for work in August the previous year. Bull was living with her mother in Praed Street, Paddington and had gone to Bayswater for a walk with Jane Newen at around 8 o'clock in the evening. There they met a girl whom Bull did not previously know. The girl told Bull she did 'a good deal of work for Mrs Stewart' and asked Bull to go with her to Stewart's house in Charlotte Street. According to *The Times* report the girl advised her to go to Stewart's and Bull went alone to Charlotte Street.

Mrs Stewart was not there and Bull returned two days later and this time found Mary Stewart at home.

When Stewart asked Bull's age, she had told her sixteen. Stewart then asked if Bull could meet with a gentleman who was not in London at the time. Bull made it clear to the judge she had gone to Mary Stewart's house for work, not to 'see a Gentleman' and had told Stewart her mother wouldn't like it. However, Bull did not mention the meeting to her mother and around a week later she returned to Charlotte Street. Here, Stewart took Bull's clothes and gave her better ones to wear; Bull had heard Stewart was going to the theatre and assumed the change of clothes was an indication she was to accompany her, but this was not the case. Mary Stewart told Bull that the gentleman who she wished Bull to meet was at the theatre, so she should wait at Stewart's house until he returned. She was taken into the drawing room reluctantly and there Stewart gave her a book to read. The 'impudent' book contained pictures. Bull's statement claimed she had 'never had connexion before with anyone'.

When the gentleman returned from the theatre, Mary Stewart arrived with wine for them all then left when the man asked her to do so. Bull then described how she had resisted the man's attempts to cajole her into bed and protested loudly until Mary Stewart returned and held her down until the man had, as *The Times* reported, 'effected my ruin'.

Bull's statement told how Stewart had said she should be paid £20 because Stewart had informed the gentleman Bull was a virgin. This the man paid Bull the following day. 'He put £20 into my Bosom. One £10 note, one £5 note and 5 sovereigns.' Bull had spent the night with the man.

Bull stayed for a week with men paying her amounts which varied from £10 to £5, all of which went to Mary Stewart. According to *The Times* report that week Bull entertained 'a great many gentlemen; as many as two a day' and was told by Stewart to always say it was her first time in order to get more money. After this episode, Bull visited Stewart's house on occasion but never to live there, having found work elsewhere.

In her statement, Bull said, 'I did not see <u>Women</u> ... there were other Girls at Mrs Stewarts...' Of 26, Charlotte Street she recounted, 'The furniture in the House was good a great deal. There were kept 3 servants, a very large house.'

When questioned by the Chairman, Bull claimed prior to working for Mary Stewart she earned her living by cleaning for a neighbour in Praed Street and she was supported by her mother, 'a monthly nurse'. Her father, Joseph Bull, was a carter working for Mr Bowyer, Cambridge Row. Bull claimed she was now, and had been, under the protection of the Society.

According to *The Times* report, the Chairman of the Middlesex Magistrates told Stewart that he had never had to pass sentence on an individual before who was in such distressing circumstances but that the Court should not allow its feelings to be influenced by anything other than justice, and:

> 'pass such a sentence as the facts of the case called for, with the hope it might act as a warning to all those who were following in the same dreadful course of conduct for which the defendant herself was about to suffer.'

He continued by saying it wasn't whether Stewart kept a house for purposes of prostitution that was the question to be answered:

> 'but whether she was one of those vile base creatures who… for the sake of filthy lucre and sordid gain had consigned to eternal perdition females of a youthful and tender age.'

Stewart was sentenced to twelve months imprisonment in Middlesex House of Correction, 'and to be kept to hard labour', at the end of which to find sureties of £300 to keep the peace, and two sureties of £150 each.

As a point of contrast, in January 1836, widowed **Ann Gwilliam** had been tried at the Middlesex Sessions and found guilty of keeping a brothel. She received a sentence of three months imprisonment in Middlesex House of Correction, and petitioned the Home Secretary for mercy, citing her innocence, an unreliable prosecution witness and the fact she was suffering from a nervous complaint amongst her grounds for clemency. Her petition was unsuccessful.

From her cell in the House of Correction, Cold Bath Fields, Mary Stewart wrote to Lord John Russell. She outlined her life story, explaining how she was born in 1800 and had been 'seduced by an officer of Rank in the Army and taken away from School by him' when she was fourteen years old. The officer was killed at the Battle of Waterloo so at fifteen she was 'thrown upon the world' without any support and, 'in a state of the utmost destitution… accepted the Protection of another officer in the Army…' Stewart lived with him for over eleven years, but when he married he left her, providing a house for her in Dorset Place, Dorset Square, London. Stewart stayed in Dorset Square for four years until 'at the request and with the assistance of some friends' she took 26, Charlotte Street and lived there for over seven years. She assured the Home Secretary:

> 'That during such period no complaint was ever made by the Police, the Parish Officers or the Neighbours against your Memorialist for the conduct of the House.'

She was arrested there on 23 May and 'ordered to find Bail for her appearance at the next Sessions herself in £200 and 2 sureties in £200 each' and finding this, was discharged.

Stewart had no forewarning of the indictment but once discharged on bail, she set about looking in to it further. She discovered that although the prosecution had been brought by the London Society for the Suppression of Juvenile Prostitution, the witness names on the back of the indictment were that of Martha Bull and a police officer, Thompson. The recognizances against her had been increased above the initial amount and her solicitor later informed her that although he had not been allowed to read the affidavit, he believed it included claims by Martha Bull that she had been trapped by Stewart in her house and been 'ravished... against her will', losing her virginity as Mary Stewart held her down. Stewart declared she was entirely innocent of the charge and when her advisors made enquiries into the character and life-style of Martha, or Patty Bull, they discovered:

> 'she was then walking the streets as a common prostitute being associated with a number of thieves and other bad characters and well-known to the Police.'

Other details ascertained meant, according to Stewart's solicitor, Bull's testimony could not be viewed with confidence by any jury.

On the morning of the trial, Stewart's solicitor had met with the counsel who had been retained to defend Stewart; Charles Phillips, senior counsel and Mr Clarkson, junior counsel. They had advised her to plead guilty to the offence of keeping a brothel, as this was true and could be easily proved. However, they advised she should be given the opportunity by the court to reply to the aggravated charge 'and that judgement would be respited for such purpose', and if the court was satisfied with her answers, then Stewart could expect a nominal punishment. On this advice, Stewart had pleaded guilty.

Charles Phillips had addressed the bench, telling them of Stewart's health situation and that the consequence of any imprisonment would be a shortening of her life. Medical certificates from three 'Medical Gentlemen' were produced and, on Stewart's behalf, Phillips:

'offered up… that she should give up the house and entirely quit the same within two days and enter to in to any recognizance the Court might impose to keep the peace'.

Because the prosecution said the case contained features of a 'very gross nature indeed' the Chairman the Magistrates and Stewart's Counsel scrutinized the Affidavit. When the prosecution objected to the suggestion that Stewart should be given time to respond to the affidavit and recognizances should be respited until the next session, the Chairman decided to call Martha Bull and examine her himself. However, he would not let the defence counsel cross-examine her directly, but would take questions and ask Bull himself. Believing the inconsistencies in Bull's version of events would be clear for everyone to hear, Stewart's counsel declined to put questions forward.

Stewart laid out the following facts to Lord John Russell. Bull's mother had been subpoenaed and it had been established her daughter was seventeen and a half at the time of the alleged 'ravishing' and not fifteen as she had claimed. This had been confirmed by a prayer book the mother had on the birth of her daughter. The first time Stewart saw Bull was when she was introduced to Stewart's house by a girl Bull called 'Cousin', Maria Jones, around twenty months before her trial. Bull was in an extremely distressed condition telling Stewart 'she was starving and could no longer keep from the Streets' and asked Stewart 'to introduce her to a Gentleman'. Stewart claimed that nothing happened on that day but she gave Bull 'some trifling relief and advised her to go to Service'. But Bull returned several times obtaining from Stewart 'trifling sums of money and cast off Clothes' whilst Stewart endeavoured to discourage her from embarking on a life of Prostitution.

Around June 1837, Bull came to Stewart's house late at night, accompanied by Maria Jones, sometimes called Maria Davis. With them was a 'Gentleman' who was unknown to Stewart's servants, and Bull asked for a bedroom where they stayed all night. Stewart was out but the following morning she saw Bull:

'who informed her that the Gentleman had given her £2 and of which she had to pay 16/- that day to the Court of Requests to save her father from being sent to Prison.'

According to Stewart this incident took place at least two months before Bull's allegation of rape, and was the first time Bull ever saw or met with a man at Charlotte Street.

A second incident took place sometime later when Bull called at Stewart's house and Bull slept with another man to whom Bull was introduced. Further visits were made with Bull sleeping with at least 15 other Gentlemen between twenty and twenty-five times over a period of many months. Some of these occasions took place after August and the last was around November 1837. Since that time, Stewart had not seen Patty Bull nor heard anything about her until she was arrested.

Stewart maintained she would not have pleaded guilty if she'd thought she would be denied an opportunity to rebut Bull's evidence and had evidence 'to prove the badness of the character of the said Patty Bull and how totally she was unworthy of belief'. Stewart claimed she was now being punished for a crime she did not commit and for which she had not faced trial, the Bench having heard only Bull's affidavit and been influenced by it, as shown in the Chairman's summing-up. Stewart had already given up running the brothel and had no further involvement with 26, Charlotte Street.

Stewart asked the Home Secretary to investigate her 'grievous Case' and said she could show Bull was working as a prostitute in Coventry Street, London, almost a year before the date of the alleged incident at Stewart's house. Bull kept the company of 'thieves and other disreputable Characters' and had returned to working as a prostitute despite the efforts of the Society who had prosecuted. Stewart requested the remainder of her sentence be remitted.

The Home Secretary then wrote to John Adams, Chairman of the Middlesex Sessions, and Adams sent a letter to Lord John Russell on 26 September 1838 informing him he was making enquiries regarding Stewart's petition.

'At his Worship's desire', Edward Jones, gaoler, wrote to Adams from the Police Office in Marylebone. The undated letter stated that George Allen and William Greenaway were taken in to custody at Marylebone and committed to the House of Correction for a month from 19 June 1837. Whilst the prisoners were at the Police Office they had been brought refreshments by several prostitutes and thieves; Bull was amongst them. Jones had then accompanied Greenaway and Allen in the Police Van to the House of Correction, and Bull had asked Jones to let her 'ride with her Bill, down to the Prison'. When asked who she meant, Bull had replied 'Bill Greenaway'. Bull's request was denied and, Jones continues, Greenaway:

'… is since transported. I know the brother and sisters they are bad characters. Martha in particular has been a Prostitute and Associate of thieves to my knowledge, from the date I mention (namely June 19 1837).'

Also at John Adams's request, Thomas Archer, the vicar of Whitchurch, Buckinghamshire, provided a copy of the baptism registration for Bull. It showed she was baptised on 20 January 1820 under the name of Patty, to her parents, Joseph and Ann. His letter and copy appears to be postmarked 5 September 1838.

In an undated statement, policemen 102 and 132 from 'D Division' confirmed Bull was 'in the habit of sleeping with a man' two months prior to the alleged rape and Mrs Willis, of Lisson Grove, could prove Bull slept with men two years ago; they were near neighbours when Bull lived in Stafford Street. Mrs Bull told Lovett, one of the policemen, Bull had been 'on the streets 2 years last July'. When Lovett went with Mrs Bull and Bull's sister to see Bull at Shepherd Street, the landlady told them she had thrown Bull out after seeing the report in *The Times* and Bull was now living next door. When visiting that house, which belonged to John Donoghue, the party found Bull with a young man. When Lovett told Bull what her neighbour had said, Bull stated she had brought the case against Mrs Stewart:

'because she would not give her £5 and that if her Man (at the same time putts her arm round the mans neck) was in trouble and she could not get money to give from the keepers of all the Houses where she had been She would indict all the f-ing Houses'.

On 19 October 1838 John Adams replied to Lord John Russell, returning Mary Stewart's petition and enclosures. He explained Stewart was mistaken in believing the Court had deviated from its usual practice regarding the examination of witnesses; Stewart had pleaded guilty and thus the Bench conducted the examination; the Defence Counsel had not put forward any 'Topics' on which the Bench should question Bull nor witnesses to counter her allegation. However, Adams was now satisfied his further enquiries had shown Bull's testimony to be 'an entire fabrication'. The fact remained that Bull's evidence was only given as aggravated circumstances in the charge to which Stewart had pleaded guilty, although it had caused the severe sentence to be passed.

Adams had made enquiries regarding the brothel Stewart ran. In a letter dated 23 September, W.E. Grimwood, Superintendent of 'E or Holborn

District' Police had reported that both 26 and 28 Charlotte Street were brothels 'but conducted very differently'. His Inspectors and Sergeants had reported 26:

> 'is still carried on in the same infamous manner as before the conviction of Mrs Stewart whose name has only been removed from the Door within these last few Days. Disturbances are frequently taking place within the House, and on the 14th of last month in consequence of Cries being heard the Serjeant in charge of that Section mounted the wall in rear of the House and heard what he has no doubt was the Mistress of the House beating one of the Girls who asked whether she (the Bawd) had not lived by her Robberies and Prostitution but as there was no Cry of Murder he did not feel himself justified in demanding Admittance. 28 Charlotte Street is conducted very quietly...'

In his letter, Adams told Lord John Russell, Stewart's 'House has been conducted in a noisy and disorderly manner, and bears a bad reputation...' but he had found no evidence or even suggestion that practices such as Bull had alleged, were taking place. He confirmed 26, Charlotte Street was now closed up, but had continued to operate for some time after Stewart was sentenced. It appeared that Stewart was the undertenant and 'hostile proceedings have been taken' against the tenant by the respectable landlord.

Adams wrote that he believed 'the Bench would have considered a sentence of six months imprisonment a full punishment as the case now stands upon investigation...' but deferred to the Home Secretary's judgement in considering whether Stewart's 'dreadful disease... and the approach of the winter' might see justice satisfied by discharging her at the end of four months, 13 November, with the required large sureties. He was also of the opinion that the Society for the Suppression of Juvenile Prostitution had been negligent and 'I respectfully submit to Your Lordship' he might consider discharging husband and wife, **John and Mary Hackwell**. The Hackwells had received a sentence of nine months imprisonment when convicted on 8 June 1838 of keeping a brothel. Adams pointed out this was:

> 'on the aggravated case proved by Martha Bull and another Girl named Jane Noon, who it appears is a very abandoned Character...'

He suggested this sentence be reduced to six months, freeing them on 8 December 1838. Lord John Russell agreed with John Adams's proposal and on 23 November, the Hackwells' sentence was reduced with sureties.

On 24 September Thomas Stirling, Clerk to the Visiting Magistrates, House of Correction Cold Bath Fields, had forwarded to the Home Office, a medical certificate for Mary Stewart 'who is confined in this Prison', in response to an enquiry from the Home Office. In a letter dated 20 August 1838, William Coulson, Surgeon at the London Lying-In Hospital and Teacher of Anatomy confirmed he had been treating Mary Stewart from 'the greatest part of last year' until June of the current one. He had also consulted with Sir Benjamin Brodie and the two had discussed an operation but Brodie was of the opinion an operation would 'hasten rather than avert her death'. He continued:

'In my opinion the confinement which Mrs Stewart is now enduring together with her distress of mind cannot fail to aggravate her complaint and consequently accelerate her end.'

A certificate dated 23 August 1838 was sent from Sir Astley Cooper (see Chapter 10). He confirmed that he had examined Stewart and had not 'the smallest doubt … her life will fall a sacrifice' to her malignant tumour. On 11 September 1838, J.P. Holmes MRCJL 'author of popular observations incident to females' confirmed he had attended Mary Stewart during the last three years and his conclusion was the same as that of William Coulson.

Thomas Wakefield, surgeon, examined Mary Stewart whilst in the House of Correction and concluded 'her Health has not suffered from her imprisonment'. His letter was dated 24 September 1838. In an undated letter William D. Cordell MRCS had advised:

'… change of Air if <u>possible</u>, the Seaside with such other means that might benefit her general health and enable her to undergo any operation…'

On 31 October 1838, Mary Stewart's sentence was reduced to four months with sureties; it is possible she died later the same year.

End Thoughts

The cases in this book are a very small sample of the petitions the Home Office received in the 1820s and the 1830s but they begin to show the variety of petitioners, their supporters or detractors and the diversity of crimes committed at this time. They also demonstrate that although advances in technology, communication and the standard of living have impacted on the way most crime is practiced today, human nature appears to remain constant and possible motivations the same; greed, naivety, desire, jealousy, a propensity to flout the rules, revenge, misunderstanding, hardship, desperation or chaotic and troubled lives.

It is heartening to see the petitions show ordinary 'strangers' who were moved to help causes, question sentences that they felt were too severe for the crime or just give people a second opportunity, for example, George Cathrow in the case of George Whitchurch, Henry Robinson Junior regarding Elizabeth Jones, and John Bennell in the case of forger William (James) Hay.

The documents also allow glimpses of what was to lie ahead, for example, industrialisation as in the petition of William Hay:

'Through the introduction of Machinery and Boys (my trade especially) there was very little opportunity for a regular journeyman to always find employment.'

Society's increasing unease with capital punishment and the need to find a different response is displayed in Henry Robinson Junior's words:

'As a banker I have too many reasons to know that embezzlement and forgery have frequently escaped with impunity from the dread of inflicting on the culprits the certain and awful fate that a prosecution would have inevitably entailed.'

Of course, the petitions and related documents only tell part of an individual's story and there are many stories out there still to be related and researched as unexpected details display the characters behind the bold facts of the case. Further examples include the vituperative letters exchanged between the committing magistrate and the local rector in the case concerning 32-year-old William Smith, who was convicted at Northampton Quarter Sessions in April 1837. Smith had destroyed his father's will whilst the executor was reading it, by throwing it on the fire. The local rector from Denford cum Ringstead petitioned for Smith's release and his sentence of seven years transportation was reduced to three months in the Penitentiary.

James Green, convicted of sheep stealing at Suffolk Quarter Sessions in March 1835, was given a pardon to enable him to give evidence for the prosecution in a murder trial.

20-year-old Mary Aldred was found guilty of breaking windows in Bulcamp House of Industry, Suffolk, in 1832. The reason for clemency proffered was that she wanted to emigrate to Australia with other local paupers, who were being sent there at the parishioners' expense. Her case was supported by them.

For other petitioners, such as Mark Guy and Matthew Hughes, their petitions almost did not reach the Home Office, in both cases for reasons of insufficient postage. At Sussex Winter Assizes, 1831, Guy had been found guilty of housebreaking. The petition which was sent the following year was overweight and, according to the Home Office file, was nearly destroyed because no-one would pay the postage. Matthew Hughes had been convicted at Liverpool Quarter Sessions in October 1837, found guilty of stealing two bales of cotton. His petition had been sent to Daniel O'Connell MP, for presentation to the Home Secretary. However, like Guy's, his petition was overweight, and was delayed en route until the outstanding postage of 4s 7d was paid. Although this situation was resolved, it appears the petition was unsuccessful and Hughes's sentence of seven years transportation, remained unchanged, on this occasion at least.

Mention must also be made of repeat-petitioner Jorgen Jorgenson about whom much has been written in other books. The Danish adventurer, gambler, writer, English spy and, for a very short time 'Protector' of Iceland was no stranger to trouble in England in the early decades of the nineteenth century and he was no stranger to Newgate prison. Jorgenson was finally transported to Van Diemen's Land, on the *Woodman* in December 1825, arriving there in April 1826. On 7 March 1835, he was pardoned on condition of never returning to Britain. His petitions, letters and some of his pamphlets are held at the National Archives.

Home Secretaries 1821–1839 (with Monarchs)

Home Secretary	Dates	Monarch
Henry Addington, 1st Viscount Sidmouth	11 June 1812– 17 January 1822	George IV (r 29 June 1820)
Robert Peel	17 January 1822– 10 April 1827	George IV
William Sturges Bourne	30 April–16 July 1827	George IV
Henry Petty-Fitzmaurice, 3rd Marquess of Lansdowne	16 July 1827– 22 January 1828	George IV
Sir Robert Peel	26 January 1828– 22 November 1830	George IV (d 26 June 1830) William IV
William Lamb, 2nd Viscount Melbourne	22 November 1830– 16 July 1834	William IV
John Ponsonby, Viscount Duncannon	19 July 1834– 15 November 1834	William IV
Arthur Wellesley, 1st Duke of Wellington	15 November 1834– 15 December 1834	William IV
Henry Goulburn	15 December 1834– 18 April 1835	William IV
Lord John Russell	18 April 1835– 30 August 1839	William IV (d 20 June 1837) Victoria
Constantine Phipps, 1st Marquess of Normanby	30 August 1839– 30 August 1841	Victoria

Appendix 2

Hulk Prison Ships

Most commonly mentioned in the petitions for Mercy, 1821–1839

Name	Location	Dates
ALONZO	Woolwich/Portsmouth	1815–1825
ANTELOPE	Bermuda	1824–1854
BELLEROPHON	Sheerness	1815–1826
CANADA hospital ship	Chatham	1826–1834
CAPTIVITY	Gosport/Devonport	1802–1817 and 1826–1834
COROMANDEL	Bermuda	1829–1854
CUMBERLAND	Chatham	1830–1833
DASHER	Woolwich	1826–1843
DISCOVERY	Woolwich/Deptford	1820–1833
DOLPHIN	Chatham	1824–1829
DROMEDARY	Woolwich/Bermuda	1825–1855
EURYALUS	Chatham/Gibraltar	1825/6–1843
*FORTITUDE**	Chatham	1833–1844
GANYMEDE	Chatham/Woolwich	1820–1838
HARDY	Portsmouth Tipner	1824–1833
HEBE	Woolwich	1839–1852
JUSTITIA	Woolwich	1815–1852
LEVEN	Woolwich/Deptford	1836–1840
LEVIATHAN	Portsmouth	1818–1844
RACOON hospital ship, attached to York hulk	Portsmouth	1826
RETRIBUTION	Woolwich/Sheerness	1803–1835
WEYMOUTH	Bermuda	1829–1836
YORK	Gosport	1820–1852

* Previously the *Cumberland*.

Extracted from The National Archives, HO17 Volunteer Support Information and The National Archives Podcast – *Prison Hulks* (Jeff James pub: 24 Feb 2012).

The National Archives, Kew, records used for prisoner-petitioners

Name	HO Number
ALLEN (ALLAN), Thomas	HO17/69/91
ARNOLD, George	HO17/69/93
ASHE, Peter (See Elizabeth Wheatley)	HO11/9/233
ATKINSON, George Forbes	HO17/43/27
BARR, Edward	HO17/43/48
	ADM 101 /43/2/3-4
BOOT, James	HO17/30/155
BROUGHTON, Edward Delves	HO17/66/97
	PCOM 2/ 205
BURGESS, William	HO17/62/46
BYRNE, Mary	HO17/55/45
CADMAN, Josiah and Sarah	HO17/49/2
	PCOM 2/195
CAINE, Thomas	HO17/93/21
CAMMEL, John	HO17/93/21
CASTLE, John	HO17/34/54
CLAGUE, John	HO17/93/21
COLLIER, William	HO17/104/65
COOKE, William	HO17/50/160
COLQUHOUN, William	HO17/93/21
CRAIG, William	HO17/24/79
DEGOUY, Joseph	HO17/48/122
DISNEY, Henry Napier (**BATTERSBY**, Arthur)	HO17/56/47
	PCOM 2/205
DUNCOMBE, Edward	HO17/85/39
EARDLEY, John	HO17/45/87
EDWARDS, Richard	HO17/60/59
ELLIS, George (**MARTIN LATKOW**, John)	HO17/49/7

(*Continued*)

Appendix 3 (*Continued*)

Name	HO Number
FANING, Edward Roger (or Rogers)	HO17/69/3
GEORGE, Robert	HO17/95/99
GIBSON, William	HO17/69/8
GLAZIER, William Richard (**GLASIER**)	HO17/69/109
GRAHAM, Thomas	HO17/52/119
GRIGG, John	HO17/67/166
	HO17/93/48
GUINEA, Gregorio	HO17/104/68
	ADM101/47/7/5
	(Folio 36)
	ADM101/47/7/2
	(Folio 4)
GWILLIAM, Ann	HO17/33/3
HACKWELL, John and Mary	HO17/38/169
HATHERELL, Isaac	HO17/4/80
HAY, William (James)	HO17/30/62
	PCOM 2/197
HEATH, Lewis and Samuel	HO17/16/6
HECTRUP, William	HO17/26/155
HIGHAM, William	HO17/132/1
HORROCKS, John	HO17/95/11
HORWOOD, Charles	HO17/19/42
HUNT, Isaac (Henry/Isaac Henry)	HO17/69/20
HUNT, Joseph	HO17/1/15
JEFFRAY, Elizabeth (**JAFFERY,** Elisabeth also surnames of Nicklson, Shafto)	HO17/80/48
JONES, Elizabeth	HO47/73/19
KAYLE, Joseph and Jane	HO17/93/21
KING, Christian	HO17/21/29
	ADM101/57/7
	Folio 3, no.5
LLOYD, Elizabeth Wood (or Betty Wood **Louther** (Lowther) **Bligh** (or **Blythe** or **Blyth**) or Elizabeth **Truss**)	HO17/81/106 PCOM 2/198
LOWRY, Alexander and **LOWRY,** John	HO17/93/21

Appendix 3 (*Continued*)

Name	HO Number
MALCOLM, Arthur	HO17/12/59
MARCOUX, John (Jean Babtiste)	HO17/104/75
McKENNIL (McKINNELL) John	HO17/60/66
MACHENERY (LILLIS/McHENREY/McHENRY) John	HO17/59/128
MONTGOMERY, John Burgh **(Col. WALLACE/Col. MORGAN)**	HO17/45/79
PASS, William	HO17/68/21
PENSON, John	HO17/55/29
REASON, Matthew (Mathew)	HO17/75/18
REYNOLDS, William Henry	HO17/30/71
	HO17/31/38
	PCOM 2/197
RICH, Charles	HO17/29/72
SPARROW, Edward	HO17/49/16
STEWART, Mary	HO17/33/133
STRANG, William	HO17/13/3
THOMPSON, Neil	HO17/33/67
TOPLEY, Thomas	HO17/49/22
VILLICUS, Antoine	HO17/33/152
WAGSTAFF, John Hill	HO17/49/71
	PCOM 2/197
WAKEFIELD, William	HO17/93/65
WEBBER, Henry	HO17/33/156
	PCOM 2/205
WHEATLEY, Elizabeth **(WEATLEY)**	HO17/69/76
	ADM101/19/6/2-7
WHITCHURCH, GEORGE	HO47/73/19
WHITE, James David	HO17/85/1
WILLIAMS, John	HO17/15/103
WISE, John	HO17/91/11
YOUNG, John	HO17/33/164
	PCOM 2/ 205

Tasmanian Archives and New South Wales Archive references for prisoner-petitioners or related prisoners

Name	Tasmanian Archives Reference	NSW State Records Convict Index
ATKINSON, George Forbes	CON 31/1/2 RGD35/1/2 No: 2679	
BATTERSBY, Arthur also known as DISNEY, Henry Napier		4/4162; Reel 944 4/4396; Reel 1019
CADMAN, Sarah (or Ann Smith, Ann Cadman) (see James Hindhaugh)		4/4444; Reel 781 Page 119 4/4479; Reel 797 Page 011 4/4081; Reel 916 4/4086; Reel 918
COLLIER, William	CON 31/1/7	
GIBSON, William	CON 18/1/6 CON 31/1/16	
GUINEA, Gregorio	CON 31/1/16 CON 18/1/16 CON 14/1/4	
HAY, William (alias James)		4/4446; Reel 781 Page 223
HECTRUP, William	CON 18/1/3 SC195-1-15-1194	
HIGHAM, William	CON 31/1/18 RGD34/1/1 No: 2944	
HINDHAUGH, James (see Sarah Cadman/ Ann Smith)		4/4060; Reel 890 4/4283 4/4061
KING, Christian		4/4476; Reel 796 Page 068–069 4/4225 Reel 965 4/4168 Reel 946

(*Continued*)

Appendix 4 (*Continued*)

Name	Tasmanian Archives Reference	NSW State Records Convict Index
LLOYD, Elizabeth Wood and name variations as Appendix 3, (also Elizabeth Wood Douglas/s) See James Westwood	CON 40/1/5 CON 45/1/1 RGD36/1/2 No:2609	
McCALLUM, Margaret (or Margaret Craig)	CON 40/1/2; CON 19/1/12	
McHENRY John or John Lillis,) name variations as Appendix 3 and Mackenery)	CON 27/1/6; CON 31/1/20	
PASS, William	CON 31/1/34; CON 18/1/8	
RICH, Charles		4/4202; Reel 957 4/4271; Reel 978 4/4472; Reel 794 Page 081-082
STRANG, William		4/4333 Reel 996
WESTWOOD, James (see Elizabeth Wood Lloyd)	CON 31/1/45 CON 23/1/3	
WHEATLEY, Elizabeth (or Ann Price, Ann Wheatley)		4/4131; Reel 933 4/4405; Reel 1022
WHEATLEY, George		4/4260; Reel 974 4/4255; Reel 973 4/4155; Reel 941 [4/4459; Reel 788 Page 109-110] [4/4480; Reel 798 Page 061]

Sources

Primary Sources:

The National Archives:

HO17	Home Office: Criminal Petitions Series 1
HO47	Home Office: Judges' Reports on Criminals
HO6	Home Office: Judges' and Recorders' Returns
HO11/9	Convict transportation registers
HO33/3	Home Office: Post Office Correspondence
PCOM 2	Home Office and Prison Commission: Newgate Prison London Register of Prisoners
ADM/101	Admiralty: Surgeons' journals

New South Wales State Archives	www.records.nsw.gov.au
Tasmanian State Archives	www.archives.tas.gov.au
The Parliamentary Archives	www.parliament.uk
Proceedings of the Old Bailey Online	www.oldbaileyonline.org
The Times Newspaper Digital Archive	www.thetimes.co.uk
Warwickshire County Record Office	www.warwickshire.gov.uk

Bibliography

ALISON, Archibald (Sir), *Principles of the Criminal Law of Scotland*, pub: William Blackwood 1832 (available as free e-book, Google).

BARROW, John Henry, (Ed), *The Mirror of Parliament for the… Session of the… Parliament of Great Britain and Ireland*, Vol 2. pub: Longman, Orme, Brown, Green & Longmans, 1839 (available as free e-book, Google).

BUCKLER, Henry, Great Britain Central Criminal Court, *Central Criminal Court Minutes of Evidence:* Pub George Herbert, 1837 (available as free e-book, Google).

ERSKINE, John, (and IVORY, James), *An Institute of the Laws of Scotland (Vol. 1)*, pub: 1824 printed for Bell & Bradfute, Edinburgh 1824) (available as free e-book, Google).

HOLFORD, George, *An Account of the General Penitentiary at Millbank*, pub: C & J Rivington, 1828 (available as free e-book, Google).

MAYHEW, Henry and **BINNY**, John, *The Criminal Prisons of London and Scenes of Prison Life*, pub: Griffin Bohn & Company, 1862 (available as free e-book, Google).

NEALE, John Preston, *Views of the Seats of Noblemen and gentlemen in England, Wales, Scotland and Ireland*, pub: Sherwood, Neeley Jones and Thomas Moule, London, 1822–9 (available as free e-book, Google).

PHILLIPS, Roderick *Untying the Knot, a short history of Divorce* pub: Cambridge University Press, 1991.

WORRALL, David, *Theatric Revolution: Drama, Censorship, and Romantic Period Subcultures 1773-1832*, pub: Oxford University Press, 2006.

The Annual Register or a View of the History and Politics of the Year (Vol 80), pub: J.G. and F. Rivington, 1839 (available as free e-book, Google).

The Gentleman's Magazine (Vol 10 and 164), Ed. A. Dodd and A. Smith, pub: W Pickering, 1838 (available as free e-book, Google).

The Gazetteer of the British Isles 9th Edition pub: John Bartholomew & Son Ltd, Edinburgh, 1966.

Webography:

The Australian Dictionary of Biography www.adb.anu.edu.au

End Notes

Chapter 1: Situating the Petitions: A Brief Overview of the 1820s and 1830s

1. *Theatric Revolution: Drama, Censorship, and Romantic Period Subcultures 1773-1832* by David Worrall pub: OUP Oxford 2006 (p 316); and *Victorian Melodramas*, Edited by James L Smith, pub: J. M. Dent & Sons Ltd, 1976 (p xix).
2. *Nineteenth Century Plays*, George Rowell, Second Edition, pub: Oxford University Press, 1982 (p1).
3. *Principles of the Criminal Law of Scotland* by (Sir) Archibald Alison, pub: William Blackwood, 1832.

Chapter 2: Bigamy

1. *Central Criminal Court Minutes of Evidence*, by Great Britain Central Criminal Court, Henry Buckler: pub George Herbert, 1837.
2. *The Annual Register of World Events: the Review of the Year, Vol 80;* ed. Edmund Burke; pub: Longmans, Green 1839.
3. *The Parliamentary Archives*, HL/PO/PB/1/1840/3&4V1n158.
4. *Untying the Knot: a Short History of Divorce* by Roderick Phillips, Cambridge University Press, 1991.
5. Old Bailey Proceedings Online (www.oldbaileyonline.org version 7.2, March 2015) April 1826 Trial of Elizabeth Wood Lloyd (t18260406-214).
6. "Australia, Tasmania, Civil Registration, 1803-1933", database with images, Family Search (https://familysearch.org/ark:/61903/1:1:Q27M-Y3KB: 26 August 2016), Elizabeth Wood Douglas, 1839.

Chapter 3: Words from the Hulks

1. The National Archives, HO17/69/84.
2. The National Archives, HO17/49/78.
3. National Archives HO17/95/99 documentation gives age as 30. Old Bailey trial notes state 36. Old Bailey Proceedings Online (www.oldbaileyonline.org version 7.2, March 2015) August 1835 Trial of Robert George (t18350817-1786).

Chapter 4: Theft

1. Old Bailey Proceedings Online (www.oldbaileyonline.org version 7.2, March 2015) May 1825 Trial of William Turner and Edward Norman (t18250519-183).

2. Old Bailey Proceedings Online (www.oldbaileyonline.org version 7.2, March 2015) January 1832 Trial of Edward Roger Faning (t18320105-8).
3. Old Bailey Proceedings Online (www.oldbaileyonline.org version 7.2, March 2015) August 1835 Trial of Robert George (t18350817-1786).
4. "Australia Births and Baptisms, 1792-1981," database, Family Search (https://familysearch.org/ark:/61903/1:1:XTC8-2BZ: 11 December 2014), Georgiana Wheatly, 07 Jul 1833; citing; FHL microfilm 993,951.
5. "Australia Marriages, 1810-1980," database, Family Search (https://family-search.org/ark:/61903/1:1:XTCY-FPK: 12 December 2014), Peter Ashe and Elizabeth Ann Or Ann Wheatley Or Price, 18 Mar 1837; citing St. Thomas, Port Macquarie, New South Wales, Australia, reference v 20-23; FHL microfilm 993,952.
6. The National Archives; GB0046 D-ECB 'Hertfordshire Archives and Local Studies' NRA 13977 March 1968.

Chapter 6: Forgery

1. Old Bailey Proceedings Online (www.oldbaileyonline.org.version 7.2, March 2015) April 1824 Trial of John Hill Wagstaff (t18240407-89).
2. Extract from Parish Register in National Archives file HO17/49/2.
3. Old Bailey Proceedings (www.oldbaileyonline.org.version 7.2, March 2015) September 1821 Trial of Josiah Cadman (t18210912-50); September 1821 Trial of Ann Smith (t18210912-51).
4. *Trewman's Exeter Flying Post or Plymouth & Cornish Advertiser*, 20 September 1821.
5. National Archives, HO6/6 'The Capital Convicts to be Reported to His Majesty in Council…'
6. National Archives, PCOM 2/195. Under Ann Smith.
7. Old Bailey Proceedings (www.oldbaileyonline.org.version 7.2, March 2015) December 1823 Trial of William alias James Hay (t18231203-43).
8. Familysearch "India Deaths and Burials, 1719-1948," database, Family Search (https://familysearch.org/ark:/61903/1:1:FGLN-ZYK: 3 December 2014), James Hay, 12 Oct 1822; citing; FHL microfilm 498,954.

Chapter 7: Words from Forgers on Forging

1. Calendar of Prisoners, Warwickshire County Records Office.
2. Warwickshire County Records Office and Handbill.

Chapter 8: Shooting and Stabbing with Intent

1. Old Bailey Proceedings (www.oldbaileyonline.org Version 7.2, March 2015) September 1830 Trial of William Hectrup (t18300916-3).

2. "Australia, Tasmania, Civil Registration, 1803-1933", database with images, Family Search (https://familysearch.org/ark:/61903/1:1:Q27M-Y3ML: 26 August 2016), William Hectriff, 1844.

3. Old Bailey Proceedings Online (www.oldbaileyonline.org, version 7.2, 01 June 2016), November 1833, Trial of Gregorio Guinea (t18331128-2).

4. "England Marriages, 1538–1973," database, Family Search. https://familysearch. org/ark:/61903/1:1:NK9P-M8N: 10 December 2014), William Henry Reynolds and Elizabeth Matilda Meadley, 10 Jun 1818; citing Saint Mary, Newington, Surrey, England, reference; FHL microfilm 307,696, 307,697, 307,698, 307,699, 307,700, 307,701, 307,702, 307,703.

5. Old Bailey Proceedings Online (www.oldbaileyonline.org, version 7.2 March 2015) January 1824, Trial of William Henry Reynolds (t18240114-1).

Chapter 11: Words from Newgate Prison, London

1. *The Criminal Prisons of London and Scenes of Prison Life*, Henry Mayhew and John Binny (pp 590).

Index